Series/Number 07-096

MAXIMUM LIKELIHOOD ESTIMATION
Logic and Practice

SCOTT R. ELIASON
University of Iowa

SAGE PUBLICATIONS
International Educational and Professional Publisher
Newbury Park London New Delhi

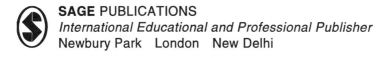

For information address:

SAGE Publications, Inc.
2455 Teller Road
Newbury Park, California 91320

SAGE Publications Ltd.
6 Bonhill Street
London EC2A 4PU
United Kingdom

SAGE Publications India Pvt. Ltd.
M-32 Market
Greater Kailash I
New Delhi 110 048 India

Printed in the United States of America

Library of Congress Catalog Card No. 89-043409

Eliason, Scott R.
Maximum likelihood estimation: logic and practice / Scott R. Eliason
p. cm.—(A Sage university papers series. Quantitative applications in the social sciences; 96)
Includes bibliographical references.
ISBN 0-8039-4107-2 (pb)
1. Social sciences—Statistical methods. 2. Estimation theory.
I. Title. II. Series: Sage university papers series. Quantitative applications in the social sciences; 07-096.
HA31.7.E45 1993
300'.01'5195—dc20 93-25529

93 94 95 96 10 9 8 7 6 5 4 3 2 1

Sage Production Editor: Susan McElroy

When citing a university paper, please use the proper form. Remember to cite the current Sage University Paper series title and include the paper number. One of the following formats can be adapted (depending on the style manual used):

(1) ELIASON, SCOTT R. (1993) Maximum Likelihood Estimation: Logic and Practice. Sage University Paper series on Quantitative Applications in the Social Sciences, 07-096. Newbury Park, CA: Sage.

OR

(2) Eliason, S. R. (1993). *Maximum likelihood estimation: Logic and practice* (Sage University Paper series on Quantitative Applications in the Social Sciences, series no. 07-096). Newbury Park, CA: Sage.

CONTENTS

SERIES EDITOR'S INTRODUCTION

Maximum likelihood (ML) estimation has been widely known in statistics at least since the 1950s, with impact of R. A. Fisher's work. However, in the social sciences, it has only rather recently gained ground as a method for estimating parameters. ML estimation systematically searches over different possible population values, finally selecting parameter estimates that are most likely (have the "maximum likelihood") to be true, given the sample observations. The leading alternative estimation procedure, of course, is ordinary least squares (OLS) regression. It is useful, then, to compare the two approaches. Suppose the simple model,

$$Y = a + bX = e,$$

where the Gauss-Markov assumptions are met and the error term is normally distributed. In this case, OLS generates best linear unbiased estimators (BLUE) of population values a and b, estimators equivalent to those generated from ML estimation.

However, in terms of estimator properties, OLS does not always fare equally when compared with ML estimation. For example, with a dichotomous dependent variable (e.g., "vote," scored 1 if a survey respondent says yes and 0 if no), OLS estimation would not be efficient, nor could the error term be normal. But a logit model, estimated with the maximum likelihood approach, could provide estimates that were asymptotically efficient and consistent, and to which significance tests are applicable. Indeed, a principal advantage of ML estimation is production of consistent and asymptotically efficient (in large samples) estimators, under conditions where OLS fails.

Because ML estimation is a general estimation procedure, it has been utilized as a means in many of our series monographs. (See, for example, the recent DeMaris paper, *Logit Modeling: Practical Applications*, No. 86). Nevertheless, until now, we have had no monograph specifically devoted to the topic. In this premier, Professor Eliason reminds the reader there are many important continuous distributions other than the normal. For instance, in an artful graphic, he employs the gamma distribution (a parent form of the exponential and chi-square) to aid in understanding the central notion of a density function. He also demonstrates that ML estimation offers a global modeling strategy capable of absorbing simple linear or complex nonlinear models. He illustrates the strategy with different examples from labor market data. (The U.S. wage distribution, with just positive values, approximates a gamma distribution.) Further, Eliason discusses different maximum likelihood statistics: the likelihood ratio test, the z test for specific parameters, the Wald test, and the entropy-based association measure R.

Carefully, Professor Eliason develops the steps to the maximum likelihood solution, including the critical selection of "start values," with helpful detail in the accompanying computer appendix on the Gauss program. At the conclusion of that section in Chapter 3, he wisely notes that "finding the maximum likelihood solution is sometimes more of an art than a science." In this long-needed introduction, he helps readers appreciate both these aspects of the ML estimation search.

—*Michael S. Lewis-Beck*
Series Editor

MAXIMUM LIKELIHOOD ESTIMATION
Logic and Practice

SCOTT R. ELIASON
University of Iowa

1. INTRODUCTION: THE LOGIC OF MAXIMUM LIKELIHOOD

Readers of the QASS series will find this monograph to be somewhat different from most monographs in this series. Why? Maximum likelihood (ML) estimation, and the principle of maximum likelihood, involves rules for obtaining estimators in models, rather than rules for constructing models per se. Thus a monograph on ML estimation will be different from one on, say, loglinear or regression models, because the latter's focus is on modeling, whereas the former's focus is on the rules for obtaining the estimators of those models. Discussion of ML estimation is more similar to a discussion of obtaining ordinary least squares or generalized least squares estimators for some linear model, rather than one on how to construct that model. However, the logic of maximum likelihood contains the seeds of a general modeling strategy that is extremely flexible and quite exciting, as it opens modeling doors that cannot be opened by most other methods.

As I show below, the normal error regression model is just one of the many models at the disposal of a researcher employing an ML framework. In an effort to combine the underlying logic and practice of ML estimation, I provide a general modeling framework utilizing the tools of maximum likelihood methods. This framework provides a very flexible modeling strategy as it accommodates cases from the simplest linear models, such as the normal error regression model, to the most complex nonlinear models linking a system of endogenous and exogenous variables with nonnormal distributions. This approach to ML estimation is similar to King's (1989). For more extensive treatments of ML estimation from a social science perspective, see King (1989), Cramer (1986), Amemiya (1985), and Maddala (1983).

Before discussing the general modeling strategy afforded us by an ML framework, I first provide in this chapter some necessary background terminology and preliminaries. I then discuss the underlying logic of ML estimation and give two simple examples to help illustrate the general technique of finding ML estimators and estimates. I close this chapter with a brief discussion on desirable properties of estimators, including those of the ML estimator.

In Chapter 2, I describe a general modeling framework using the logic of maximum likelihood. I illustrate both this framework and useful inferential tools using the normal distribution. By illustrating this framework with the normal distribution, useful extensions to the normal error regression model are facilitated. In Chapter 3, I discuss some basic techniques for finding maximum likelihood solutions. In this chapter, both the general form of the covariance matrix for ML estimates and the sampling distribution of ML estimators are given. In Chapter 4, I provide more empirical examples, moving beyond the normal distribution to other useful distributions. Finally, Chapter 5 provides some useful likelihoods that are not illustrated in Chapter 4.

Background and Preliminaries

The term *random variable* refers to some real-valued function that maps a real number to one of a number of observable outcomes. For example, a variable, say Y, with two possible outcomes given by $Y = 1$ if an individual is unemployed and $Y = 0$ if an individual is not unemployed is a random variable. A random variable may also be defined as the integer associated with the result of observing an individual in one of a number of social class positions. Both of these random variables are examples of *discrete random variables,* variables that take on either finite values or infinite but countable values.

A *continuous random variable,* on the other hand, is one that takes on an infinite number of possible values on the real number line. For example, a random variable representing the chronological age of a selected individual can be considered a continuous random variable. Other examples of continuous random variables include some types of rewards, such as labor market wages. By convention, a Roman capital letter is used to denote the random variable and the corresponding lowercase letter is used to denote an empirical observation derived from the random variable.

Each possible outcome associated with a random variable has a corresponding probability of occurrence. This probability may be written as a function mapping each value or range of values for a random variable to a corresponding probability of occurrence. This function is known either as a *probability function* (PF) for discrete random variables or as a *probability density function* (PDF) for continuous random variables. For example, assume a random variable X_i defined such that $X_i = 1$ if individual i has a managerial occupation and $X_i = 0$ otherwise. In other words, assume X to be a dummy variable indicating whether or not an individual has a managerial occupation. Now with a sample of size N, define a new random variable Y such that $Y = \Sigma_{i=1}^{N} X_i$. The new random variable Y has a PF written

$$\mathrm{P}(Y = y; N, p) = \binom{N}{y} p^y (1-p)^{N-y} \qquad y = 0, 1, 2, \ldots, N, \; 0 \le p \le 1 . \qquad (1.1)$$

with y being the number of individuals in the sample who have managerial occupations (i.e., those with $X_i = 1$) and p being a parameter giving the probability that any one individual might have a managerial occupation in the population. This PF is the binomial probability function, given here specifically as the sum of N Bernoulli random variables. The binomial PF is useful when one is modeling some dichotomous variable. Another useful PF, the multinomial PF, generalizes the binomial PF and is used for modeling polytomous variables. I discuss, and provide an example of, the multinomial PF in Chapter 4.

A well-known PDF for a continuous random variable is the normal distribution; this may be written as

$$\mathrm{f}(y; \mu, \sigma^2) = \frac{1}{\sqrt{2\pi\sigma^2}} \exp\left[\frac{-(y-\mu)^2}{2\sigma^2}\right] \qquad -\infty < y < +\infty, \qquad (1.2)$$

$$-\infty < \mu < +\infty, \; 0 < \sigma^2 < +\infty$$

where y gives observations on the random variable Y, and μ and σ^2 are parameters governing the location and shape of the distribution, respectively. For the normal distribution, the random variable Y may take on values over the entire real number line. Figure 1.1 shows the normal distribution with zero mean, that is, $\mu = 0$, and different values of σ^2,

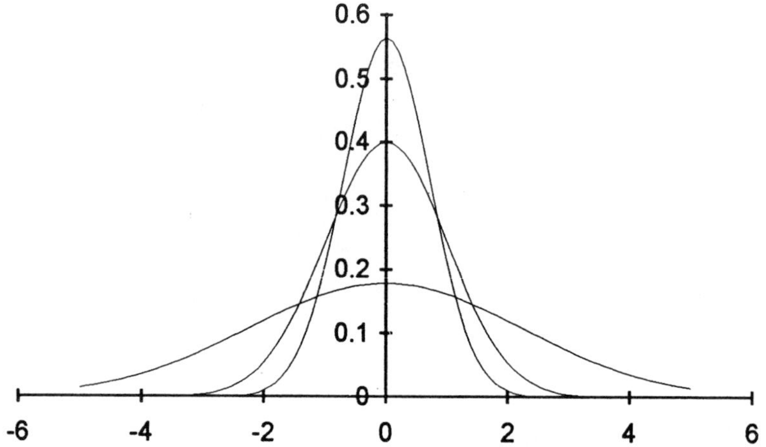

Figure 1.1. Normal Distribution for $\mu = 0$ and, From Highest Peeked Distribution to Lowest, $\sigma^2 = 0.5, 1, 5$
NOTE: Vertical axis is $f(y; \mu, \sigma^2)$; horizontal axis is Y.

the variance of the distribution. The normal distribution is useful when we posit a model for some continuous random variable that has either constant variance or nonconstant variance that itself can be modeled. I show this in some of the examples below.

Although the normal distribution is a very useful PDF, other continuous distributions are better suited for properties of continuous variables in the social sciences. For example, labor market rewards (e.g., wages and income) consist entirely of nonnegative real values, the empirical distribution of which is consistently right-skewed. A very flexible continuous distribution that is primarily used for waiting time models, but is applicable for any nonnegative continuous random variable, is the gamma PDF.

The functional form of the gamma PDF can be daunting:

$$f(y; \mu, \nu) = \left(\frac{1}{\Gamma(\nu)}\right)\left(\frac{\nu}{\mu}\right)^{\nu} y^{(\nu-1)} \exp\left(\frac{-\nu y}{\mu}\right) \tag{1.3}$$

$$0 \le y < +\infty;\ 0 < \mu < +\infty;\ 0 < \nu < +\infty\ .$$

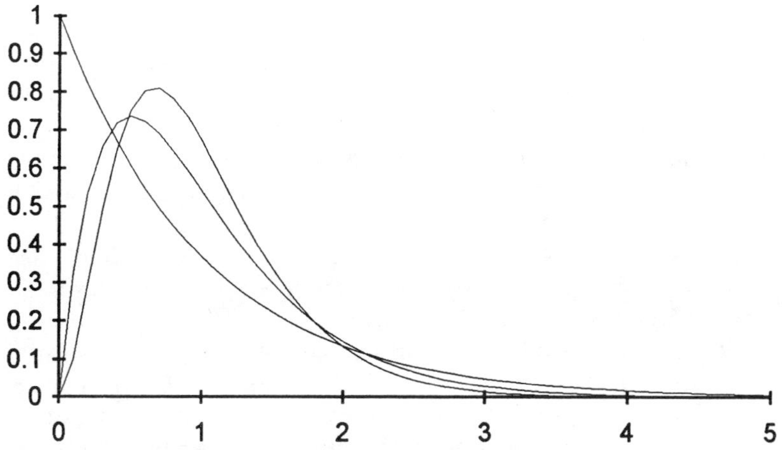

Figure 1.2. Gamma Distribution for $\mu = 1$ and $\nu = 1, 2$, and 3
NOTE: Vertical axis is $f(y; \mu, \nu)$; horizontal axis is Y.

However, it is an extremely flexible distribution, as can be seen in Figures 1.2 and 1.3. For the gamma distribution, μ governs the location of the distribution (i.e., μ is the mean of the gamma distribution) and

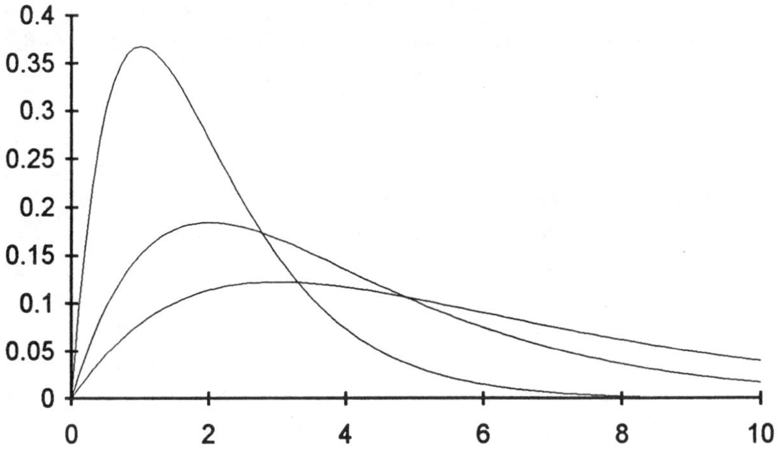

Figure 1.3. Gamma Distribution for $\mu = 2, 4$, and 6, and $\nu = 2$
NOTE: Vertical axis is $f(y; \mu, \nu)$; horizontal axis is Y.

the ratio μ^2/ν governs the shape (i.e., μ^2/ν is the variance). For distributions with $\nu = 1$, the gamma distribution becomes the exponential distribution; when both $\nu = 1$ and $\mu = 1$, the gamma distribution becomes the standard exponential distribution. The well-known chi-square distribution with n degrees of freedom is also a specific form of the gamma distribution with $\mu = n$ and $\nu = n/2$. Finally, for $\mu = 1$ and $\nu = 2$, the gamma distribution is a good approximation of the wage distribution in the United States. As I show in the examples below, the gamma distribution is useful when we have a model for a nonnegative continuous random variable that has a nonconstant variance dependent on the mean, but a constant coefficient of variation.

For maximum likelihood estimation, as well as in other estimation procedures, the first and second moments of a given PDF or PF are of specific interest. First, considerable interest lies in estimation of the first moment of a distribution, or the mean. The mean of a PDF or PF (not to be confused with the sample mean) for a random variable Y is denoted as $E(Y)$, read *the expected value of Y*. For heuristic purposes, $E(Y)$ can be thought of as some best guess of the value of Y. The expected value of a random variable indicates the central location of the mass or central tendency of the distribution.

Not only is the central tendency of interest, so too is the degree of variability, or variance, in the PDF or PF. This is related to the second moment of the distribution. For a specific random variable Y, $V(Y)$ denotes *the variance of the distribution of Y* (not to be confused with the sample variance). The variance of the distribution of Y indicates the degree of dispersion or uncertainty in Y.

Often we may write a distribution in a form such that $E(Y)$ and $V(Y)$ can be easily viewed as functions of the parameters in a PDF or PF. For example, in the normal distribution, $E(Y) = \mu$ and $V(Y) = \sigma^2$. For the gamma PDF, $E(Y) = \mu$ and $V(Y) = \mu^2/\nu$. For the binomial PF, $E(Y) = Np$ and $V(Y) = Np(1 - p)$. Thus a model for $E(Y)$ will usually correspond to a model for the parameter governing the central location of a distribution. For example, in the normal PDF, a model of $E(Y)$ always corresponds to the same model for μ. Similarly, a model for $V(Y)$ will correspond to some model derived from the parameter or parameters governing the variance of a distribution. For example, in the normal PDF, a model for $V(Y)$ corresponds to the same model for σ^2.

Typically, we are interested in modeling $E(Y)$, or sometimes both $E(Y)$ and $V(Y)$, conditional on a set of fixed factors, independent variables, or regressors. In maximum likelihood estimation, these models correspond to models of parameters governing a specified PDF or PF. As is conventional in most statistical texts, a *parameter* is simply defined as any constant in a PF or PDF that can take on some arbitrary value within a specified range. As mentioned above, PDF and PF parameters govern various behaviors of the PDF or PF.

Probably the most common model for continuous random variables in the social sciences is the linear regression model for $\boldsymbol{\mu}$ in the normal PDF. Without present consideration for subscripts, this model may be written simply as

$$\boldsymbol{\mu} = \boldsymbol{X\beta}, \tag{1.4}$$

which is equivalent to

$$\mathrm{E}(\boldsymbol{Y}) = \boldsymbol{X\beta} \tag{1.5}$$

in the normal PDF, where $\boldsymbol{X}$ typically denotes a matrix of fixed factors and $\boldsymbol{\beta}$ a vector of *model parameters.* When a distinction is necessary, I refer to parameters that are part of a model structure as *model parameters* and parameters that are explicitly part of some PDF (PF) as *PDF (PF) parameters.* When no distinction is necessary I simply use the term *parameter* to mean both types. Because appropriate modeling strategies depend on the PDF or PF being used, I discuss such strategies in more detail below.

The Principle of Maximum Likelihood

In the social sciences, data are used both to test hypotheses and to aid in theory construction. The principle of maximum likelihood, due to the work of the distinguished statistician R. A. Fisher (1950), provides a statistical framework for assessing wisely the information available in the data. Suppose we have N independent and identically distributed (iid) random variables denoted $\boldsymbol{Y} = [Y_1, \ldots, Y_N]'$ in column vector notation, a corresponding column vector of observed data $\boldsymbol{y} = [y_1, \ldots, y_N]'$ drawn from $\boldsymbol{Y}$, and a joint PDF or PF given by $\mathrm{f}(\boldsymbol{y};\boldsymbol{\theta})$ with p unknown PDF/PF parameters denoted as a column vector $\boldsymbol{\theta} = [\theta_1, \ldots, \theta_p]'$. (Note that $\boldsymbol{\theta}$ may be a scalar with $p = 1$.) The principle of maximum likelihood can be stated as follows: Find an estimate for $\boldsymbol{\theta}$ such that it maximizes the likelihood of observing those data that were actually observed. In other words, given a sample of observations $\boldsymbol{y}$ for the random vector $\boldsymbol{Y}$, find a solution for $\boldsymbol{\theta}$ that maximizes the joint probability density function or joint probability function, $f(\boldsymbol{y};\boldsymbol{\theta})$.

Because the elements in $\boldsymbol{Y}$ are independent, the joint distribution may be written as the product of the individual marginal distributions. We then maximize what is commonly called the likelihood function,[1]

$$\Lambda(\boldsymbol{\theta}) = \prod_{i=1}^{N} f(y_i;\, \boldsymbol{\theta})\,. \tag{1.6}$$

where $\Pi_{i=1}^{N}$ is the product operator. Working with products results in considerable computational difficulties; summations, on the other hand, are more tractable. With the natural log of $\Lambda(\boldsymbol{\theta})$ being an increasing function of $\Lambda(\boldsymbol{\theta})$ over its entire range, we instead maximize the log-likelihood function $\ln[\Lambda(\boldsymbol{\theta})] = \lambda(\boldsymbol{\theta})$, obtaining the same solution as we would by maximizing $\Lambda(\boldsymbol{\theta})$. Given the iid assumption, $\lambda(\boldsymbol{\theta})$ may be written

$$\lambda(\boldsymbol{\theta}) = \ln\left[\prod_{i=1}^{N} f(y_i;\, \boldsymbol{\theta})\right] = \sum_{i=1}^{N} \ln[f(y_i;\, \boldsymbol{\theta})]. \tag{1.7}$$

The solution for $\boldsymbol{\theta}$ that maximizes the log-likelihood function in Equation 1.7 is called the maximum likelihood estimator (MLE), typically denoted $\hat{\boldsymbol{\theta}}$, the value of which is called the maximum likelihood estimate.

To see how this is done, a simple illustration using the normal distribution should prove helpful. Assume we are interested in finding a value for μ, the mean of the normal distribution, which maximizes the log-likelihood for a specific set of data and a given value for σ^2. Assume further that we have randomly sampled 10 individuals from the labor force who are working and recorded each individual's per hour wage. It should be emphasized that a sample size of 10 is useful only for heuristic purposes. In the typical ML estimation procedure, one would want to have a large sample size because the desirable properties of the MLE (to be discussed below) are justified only in large sample situations.[2]

Because we are assuming a normal distribution in this example, and because per hour wages are notoriously right-skewed, using the natural log of wages helps to normalize this empirical distribution. Assume that the observed vector of log of per hour wages is given as

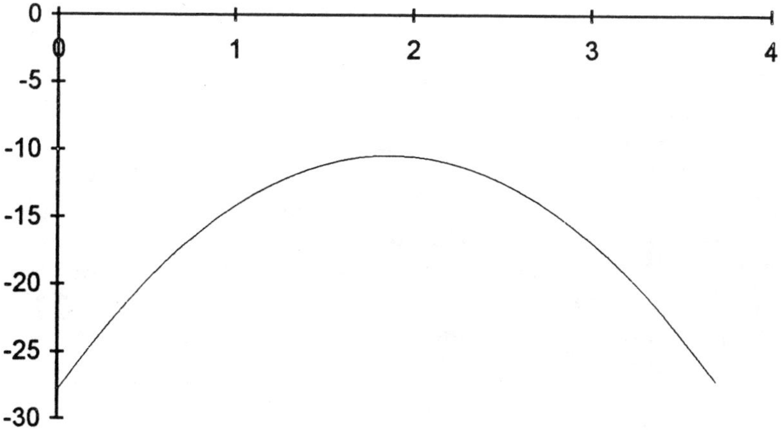

Figure 1.4. Log-Likelihood for the Normal Distribution
NOTE: Vertical axis is the log-likelihood; horizontal axis is μ.

$$y = [1.91, 1.54, 1.71, 1.55, 3.02, 1.76, 2.50, 1.84, 1.61, 1.25]'.$$

Figure 1.4 gives values for the log-likelihood function for the normal distribution (given in Equation 1.8, described below) on the vertical axis and values for μ on the horizontal axis using these data. As we trace from left to right on the horizontal axis, we find that the log-likelihood function first begins to rise, reaches a maximum, and then falls off. Tracing the log-likelihood in this manner can help to give us an intuitive feel for how the MLE is found in this case. Recall that we are looking for a specific value for μ that maximizes the log-likelihood function. Clearly, this function has a maximum, as we can see by tracing it as just described. Further, we can see that the maximum for this case is unique, that is, there is no more than one peak in this distribution. As we trace the values for μ on the horizontal axis, we find that the function reaches a maximum around $\mu = 1.87$ and is given by -10.40. By using this graphic approach, we find that the maximum likelihood estimate for μ is 1.87 in this example. That is, choosing a value of 1.87 for μ in this case maximizes the likelihood of observing the data vector $\boldsymbol{y}$.

We could construct a graph and find the MLE for the mean of a normal distribution, μ, in the manner just described for each new set of data. However, this would be tedious and time-consuming, and not always quite so precise. By using the tools afforded us by calculus we can construct a formula that will tell us how to calculate the MLE for μ in the normal distribution for all sets of data and with a degree of precision that is unobtainable by graphic techniques.

Assume we have a sample of size N drawn from $\boldsymbol{Y}$, an $N \times 1$ iid normal random vector as described above. Here we write $\boldsymbol{Y} \sim \mathrm{N}(\mu,\sigma^2)$ to represent the normal PDF and read "$\boldsymbol{Y}$ is normally distributed with parameters μ and σ^2." Recall that in the normal PDF, μ governs the central tendency or mean of the distribution, and σ^2 governs the dispersion or variance. As in the graphic example in Figure 1.4, assume that σ^2 is known and that the parameter vector is only a scalar such that $\boldsymbol{\theta} = [\mu]$, and $f(\boldsymbol{y};\boldsymbol{\theta}) = f(\boldsymbol{y};\mu)$. The log-likelihood $\lambda(\mu)$ is then given by

$$\lambda(\mu) = \sum_{i=1}^{N} \ln\left[\frac{1}{\sqrt{2\pi\sigma^2}} \exp\left(\frac{-(y_i - \mu)^2}{\sigma^2}\right)\right] \tag{1.8}$$

$$= -N(\ln\sqrt{2\pi\sigma^2}) - \frac{1}{2\sigma^2}\sum_{i=1}^{N}(y_i - \mu)^2$$

where the y_i are the observations on $\boldsymbol{Y}$. The quantity $-N(\ln\sqrt{2\pi\sigma^2})$ does not depend on the y_i and may be disregarded for now. Further, $1/(2\sigma^2)$, a constant scaling factor, may also be disregarded for now because σ^2 is assumed known. The relevant portion, or kernel, of the log-likelihood is

$$-\sum_{i=1}^{N}(y_i - \mu)^2 . \tag{1.9}$$

To find the MLE for μ using the information given in Equation 1.9, we must have a way to find the maximum in a graph like that in Figure 1.4 for all possible combinations of the data vector and μ. The most useful way to accomplish this is by imagining a set of tangent lines to the curve of the log-likelihood function as is shown in Figure 1.5. Each tangent line on the curve has a slope associated with it. We can note that the slope of the line that is tangent to the solution point—that is, the maximum—is 0. That is, the tangent line at the maximum is a horizontal

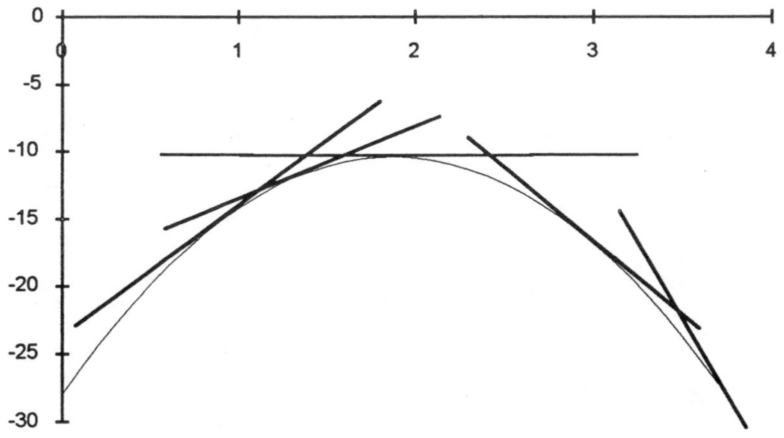

Figure 1.5. Log-Likelihood for the Normal Distribution With Tangent Lines
NOTE: Vertical axis is the log-likelihood; horizontal axis is μ.

line. Fortunately, this holds for all possible combinations of the data vector and μ. That is, the maximum likelihood solution can be found at the point on the log-likelihood curve at which the tangent line has zero slope.

To find this point without recourse to graphic techniques, we take the first derivative of Equation 1.9 with respect to μ, set it to zero, and solve for μ. The first derivative represents the slope of the lines tangent to the log-likelihood as shown in Figure 1.5. By setting the first derivative to zero, we are setting the slope of the tangent line to zero, and thus forcing it to be a horizontal line. Then, by solving this formula, we find the point at which a tangent line with zero slope touches the curve. In this case, that point will be the maximum likelihood solution for μ in the normal PDF.

Once this is done, however, we need to verify that the solution is indeed a maximum rather than a minimum whose tangent line slope would also be zero. This is done by checking the second derivative of the log-likelihood with respect to the parameter of interest, which tells us whether the curve is concave up or down around the solution. If the second derivative is less than zero, then the curve is concave down (as in Figure 1.5) and the solution is then a maximum.

Taking the first derivative of the kernel of the log-likelihood with respect to μ we have

$$\frac{\partial}{\partial\mu}\left[-\sum_{i=1}^{N}(y_i-\mu)^2\right]=2\sum_{i=1}^{N}y_i-2N\mu\,. \tag{1.10}$$

Taking the result in Equation 1.10, setting it to zero, and solving for μ gives the MLE for μ,

$$\hat{\mu}=\frac{\sum_{i=1}^{N}y_i}{N}\,. \tag{1.11}$$

With the second derivative of the log-likelihood in Equation 1.8 with respect to μ being $-N/\sigma^2$, we indeed have a maximum because $-N/\sigma^2$ is always less than zero. Therefore, the MLE for μ in the normal distribution, $\hat{\mu}$, is the sample mean. If we calculate the sample mean for *y*, we find that it is 1.87, which was the solution obtained from examining the graph in Figure 1.4.

It is often desirable also to obtain the variance of the maximum likelihood estimator. In so doing, the second derivative comes into play once again. As I show in more detail below, the variance of the MLE can always be given as a function of the second derivative. When we are dealing with more than one parameter in a parameter vector, the variance-covariance matrix for the MLE of the parameter vector is given as a function of the matrix of second derivatives. This matrix of second derivatives is typically called the *Hessian matrix*; it is discussed in more detail below.

As mentioned above, the second derivative of the log-likelihood with respect to μ is $-N/\sigma^2$. For our one-parameter example here, the variance of $\hat{\mu}$, $V(\hat{\mu})$, is then given by

$$V(\hat{\mu})=\left[-E\left(\frac{\partial^2\lambda(\mu)}{\partial\mu\partial\mu}\right)\right]^{-1}=\sigma^2/N\,. \tag{1.12}$$

The intermediate step in Equation 1.12 is the mathematical form of the previously mentioned function of the second derivative. Specifically, it is the inverse of the negative expected value of the second derivative. As $\hat{\mu}$ is simply the sample mean, it is not surprising that the variance of $\hat{\mu}$ turns out to be the usual form for the variance of the sample mean.

If we wish to use Equation 1.12 to conduct either the usual z test for the mean or to construct the usual confidence interval around the mean, we need to replace σ^2 with an estimate. The maximum likelihood estimator for σ^2 is the sample variance,

$$\hat{\sigma}^2 = \frac{\sum_{i=1}^{N} (y_i - \hat{\mu})^2}{N} . \tag{1.13}$$

It is well known that $\hat{\sigma}^2$ is a biased estimator for σ^2. (I discuss in more detail what a biased estimator is below.) To correct the bias, we multiply $\hat{\sigma}^2$ by $N/(N - 1)$. Thus, as the sample size grows large, the bias in $\hat{\sigma}^2$ becomes inconsequential. For this example, $\hat{\sigma}^2 = 0.24$ and $V(\hat{\mu}) = 0.24/10 = 0.024$.

The previous example is a bit simplistic. We are rarely interested in only the marginal information of the random variable $\boldsymbol{Y}$ found in the data. Often we are interested in modeling $\boldsymbol{Y}$ conditional on a set of fixed independent variables, say $\boldsymbol{X}$. Let $\boldsymbol{Y}$ be an $N \times 1$ vector of iid random variables with a conditional normal distribution given some function of $\boldsymbol{X}$, say $g(\boldsymbol{X})$. Further, let $\boldsymbol{X}$ be an $N \times p$ matrix with $\boldsymbol{x}_i$ being a $1 \times p$ vector of values for the ith row in $\boldsymbol{X}$. Note that the first column in $\boldsymbol{X}$ is 1 for all i to fit the usual constant term in the model. As above, let y_i be the value of Y_i for case i.

To make the condition on $\boldsymbol{X}$ explicit in the PDF of $\boldsymbol{Y}$, we write $\boldsymbol{Y} \sim N[g(\boldsymbol{X}),\sigma^2]$. This is the same as stating that $\boldsymbol{Y}$ is distributed as a normal random variable with $E(\boldsymbol{Y}) = \boldsymbol{\mu} = g(\boldsymbol{X})$ and $V(\boldsymbol{Y}) = \sigma^2$. To bring out the elements more explicitly, we may write this relationship as $E(Y_i) = \mu_i = g(\boldsymbol{x}_i)$. Note that $V(Y_i) = \sigma^2$ is a constant in this example and does not depend on $\boldsymbol{X}$. This notation is useful because it makes clear that $\boldsymbol{Y}$ is conditionally normal with μ conditioned on some function of $\boldsymbol{X}$.

To simplify matters at this point, assume that we have only one independent variable. For example, assume that along with the log of per hour wages, we also collected data on the years of completed schooling for each case in the previous example. Denote this independent variable as $\boldsymbol{x}_1$ with

$$\boldsymbol{x}_1 = [15, 12, 12, 11, 18, 16, 16, 14, 12, 12]'.$$

Further assume that we are interested in modeling the log of per hour wages conditional on years of schooling completed. If we let $g(\boldsymbol{x}_1)$ be linear in $\boldsymbol{x}_1$ such that $g(\boldsymbol{x}_1) = \beta_0 + \beta_1\boldsymbol{x}_1$, where β_0 and β_1 are model parameters, then the relationship between $E(\boldsymbol{Y})$ and $\boldsymbol{x}_1$ can now be written as

$$E(Y_i) = \mu_i = \beta_0 + \beta_1 x_{1i}\,. \tag{1.14}$$

This model is equivalent to the simple linear regression model with normally distributed errors (Neter, Wasserman, & Kutner, 1985). That is, when $\boldsymbol{Y}$ is assumed to be normally distributed given $\boldsymbol{x}_1$, Equation 1.14 is equivalent to the model written

$$y_i = \beta_0 + \beta_1 x_{1i} + \varepsilon_i, \tag{1.15}$$

where ε_i is normally distributed with $E(\varepsilon_i) = 0$ and $V(\varepsilon_i) = \sigma^2$. It is worth emphasizing that models 1.14 and 1.15 are exactly the same because of the position of μ relative to $\boldsymbol{y}$ in the normal PDF. In general, 1.14 and 1.15 will not be equivalent when other PDFs or PFs are used (e.g., see Chapter 4).

With $\mu_i = \beta_0 + \beta_1 x_{1i}$, we replace μ in Equation 1.8 with $\beta_0 + \beta_1 x_{1i}$ and write it as

$$-N(\ln\sqrt{2\pi\sigma^2}) - \frac{1}{2\sigma^2}\sum_{i=1}^{N}(y_i - \beta_0 - \beta_1 x_{1i})^2\,. \tag{1.16}$$

As in the previous example, we can try to obtain an intuitive sense for finding the maximum likelihood solution by examining a graph of the log-likelihood surface. This time, however, the graph requires three dimensions—one for possible values of β_0, one for possible values of β_1, and one for the values of the log-likelihood.

Figure 1.6 gives the log-likelihood surface using the example data. As in the previous example, the maximum likelihood solution appears where the log-likelihood surface obtains its maximum height. However, given that we are now in three dimensions, finding the solution point graphically is not as easy as in two dimensions. It appears clear that the solution can be found at the peak of the log-likelihood surface in the middle of the graph, but being precise is another matter. All that we can tell from the perspective of Figure 1.6 is that the solution for the slope, β_1, appears to fall close to the first hatch-mark to the right of zero on the β_1 axis. This corresponds roughly to a value of $1/7$ or approximately 0.14. From this perspective,

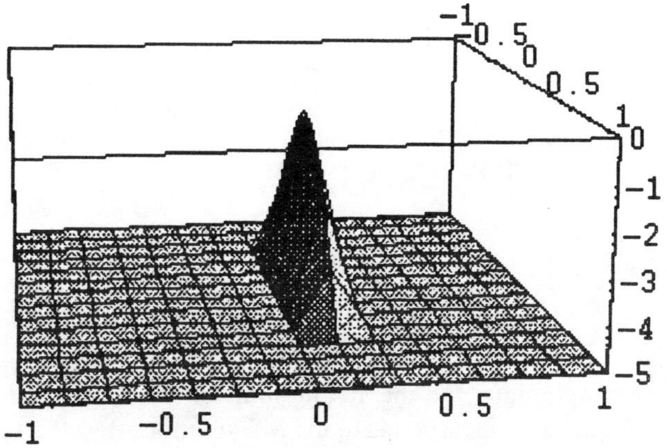

Figure 1.6. Log-Likelihood Surface for a Simple Regression
NOTE: Axis numbered along the top is β_0, the constant term. Axis numbered along the bottom is β_1, the slope. Axis numbered down the right side is the log-likelihood.

however, it is not at all clear what the value of the constant term, β_0, might be. Because graphic techniques are not always reliable, we desire a method to obtain the solutions in a more precise and reliable way.

As we did above, to find the solution more precisely, we take the first derivative of the log-likelihood in Equation 1.16 with respect to each model parameter separately, set the resulting equations to zero, and solve for the corresponding parameter. To do this, first note that only the part in Equation 1.16 that depends on both the data and the model parameters is of interest:

$$-\sum_{i=1}^{N}(y_i - \beta_0 - \beta_1 x_{1i})^2 . \tag{1.17}$$

Maximizing Equation 1.17 is equivalent to minimizing

$$\sum_{i=1}^{N}(y_i - \beta_0 - \beta_1 x_{1i})^2 = \sum_{i=1}^{N}\varepsilon_i^2 , \tag{1.18}$$

the sum of squared errors, which gives us OLS estimators for the $\boldsymbol{\beta}$. This leads to the well-known result that when we specify $\boldsymbol{Y} \sim \text{N}(\beta_0 + \beta_1\boldsymbol{x}_1, \sigma^2)$,

ML and OLS estimates for the model parameters will be the same. Specifically,

$$\hat{\beta}_1 = \frac{\sum_{i=1}^{N} (x_i - \bar{x})(y_i - \bar{y})}{\sum_{i=1}^{N} (x_i - \bar{x})^2} \quad \text{and} \quad \hat{\beta}_0 = \bar{y} - \hat{\beta}_1 \bar{x} .$$

For the example data, the maximum point on the likelihood surface given in Figure 1.6 corresponds to the ML solutions $\hat{\beta}_1 = 0.19$ and $\hat{\beta}_0 = -0.75$.

In general, for a multiple regression model with $\boldsymbol{\mu} = \boldsymbol{X\beta}$, where $\boldsymbol{\mu}$ is now an $N \times 1$ vector of expected values for $\boldsymbol{Y}$, $\boldsymbol{X}$ is defined as above, and $\boldsymbol{\beta}$ is now a $p \times 1$ vector of model parameters, we find the ML solution in a similar manner. Except now, however, graphic techniques, heuristic or otherwise, are essentially useless as we have a p-dimensional log-likelihood surface from which to obtain a maximum. Although graphic techniques are of no use, the tools afforded us by calculus for finding the maximum still apply.

To find the ML estimates for the multiple linear regression model assuming normality, we need to obtain the first derivatives of the log-likelihood with respect to $\boldsymbol{\beta}$, set this result to 0, and then solve for $\boldsymbol{\beta}$. For the general case, the log-likelihood may be written as

$$\lambda(\beta) = -N(\ln\sqrt{2\pi\sigma^2}) - \frac{1}{2\sigma^2}\sum_{i=1}^{N} (y_i - \boldsymbol{x}_i\boldsymbol{\beta})^2 , \tag{1.19}$$

where $\boldsymbol{x}_i$ is the ith row in $\boldsymbol{X}$. For a specified element in $\boldsymbol{\beta}$, say β_k, and the corresponding column in $\boldsymbol{X}$, $\boldsymbol{x}_k$, the first derivative can be written

$$\frac{\partial\lambda(\boldsymbol{\beta})}{\partial\beta_k} = \sigma^{-2}\sum_{i=1}^{N} x_{ik}(y_i - \boldsymbol{x}_i\boldsymbol{\beta}) . \tag{1.20}$$

Setting this derivative to zero and solving for $\boldsymbol{\beta}$ gives the ML solution for the general case:

$$\hat{\boldsymbol{\beta}} = (\boldsymbol{X}'\boldsymbol{X})^{-1}\boldsymbol{X}'\boldsymbol{Y}. \tag{1.21}$$

This is also the OLS solution for the parameter vector $\boldsymbol{\beta}$. This demonstrates that when $\boldsymbol{Y} \sim \mathrm{N}(\boldsymbol{X\beta},\sigma^2)$, OLS estimators and ML estimators for the $\boldsymbol{\beta}$ are equivalent.

Although we already know that this is the maximum likelihood solution, it is still instructive to check this using the second derivatives, as was done for the previous example. To do so we first take the second derivative of the log-likelihood with respect to $\boldsymbol{\beta}$,

$$\frac{\partial^2\lambda(\boldsymbol{\beta})}{\partial\boldsymbol{\beta}\partial\boldsymbol{\beta}} = \boldsymbol{X}'\boldsymbol{X}(-\sigma^{-2}) \,. \tag{1.22}$$

Because $\boldsymbol{X}'\boldsymbol{X}$ must be a positive definite matrix and σ must always be positive, the matrix of second derivatives is negative definite, which tells us that Equation 1.21 constitutes a maximum rather than a minimum. Therefore, Equation 1.21 is indeed the maximum likelihood solution.

Finally, as with the previous example, we can use the result in Equation 1.22 to obtain the variance-covariance matrix for $\hat{\boldsymbol{\beta}}$. Recall that the variance of the MLE will be the inverse of the negative expected value of the matrix of second derivatives. Thus

$$\mathrm{V}(\hat{\boldsymbol{\beta}}) = (\boldsymbol{X}'\boldsymbol{X})^{-1}\sigma^2, \tag{1.23}$$

which is the same *form* as the OLS solution. However, the ML estimator for σ^2 is not the same as the unbiased estimator used with OLS methods. This bias is a function of the ratio $N/(N-p)$, where p is the number of model parameters. For a fixed p, the bias becomes inconsequential as the sample size grows large.

For this example, replacing σ^2 with the ML estimator

$$\hat{\sigma}^2 = \frac{\sum_{i=1}^{N} \varepsilon_i^2}{N} = 0.065\,,$$

Equation 1.23 gives the ML estimates of the covariance matrix as

$$\hat{V}(\hat{\boldsymbol{\beta}}) = \begin{bmatrix} 0.256 & -0.018 \\ -0.018 & 0.001 \end{bmatrix}.$$

As usual, the variances of the parameter estimates are given on the diagonal—$\hat{V}(\hat{\beta}_0) = 0.256$ and $\hat{V}(\hat{\beta}_1) = 0.001$—and the covariances are given on the off-diagonal—$\hat{V}(\hat{\beta}_0, \hat{\beta}_1) = -0.018$. These values may be used to construct the usual confidence intervals for model estimates and for hypothesis tests of model parameters. However, because this example with 10 cases was given primarily to illustrate the logic of finding the ML solution, and because ML estimators have desirable properties in large samples, I defer detailed discussion and illustration of interval estimation and hypothesis testing to later in the monograph.

Desirable Properties of Estimators

Once we obtain any type of estimator, it is useful to know its properties. How close does it come to the true value of the parameter that we wish to know? With how much precision is it estimated? There are many properties that may be used to judge the quality of one estimator over another, and an in-depth discussion is beyond the scope of the current monograph (see Amemiya, 1985, for a more thorough discussion). However, three properties of estimators—unbiasedness, consistency, and efficiency—warrant discussion.

The property of *unbiasedness,* briefly mentioned above, is useful in small sample situations. For some parameter θ, if an estimator $\tilde{\theta}$ is such that $E(\tilde{\theta}) = \theta$, then that estimator is said to be an unbiased estimator of the parameter θ. In other words, if the expected value of the estimator equals the parameter, then it is an unbiased estimator of that parameter.

Another very important property is *consistency.* For some estimator $\tilde{\theta}$ of θ, if the limit as the sample size tends toward infinity is such that

$$\lim_{n \to \infty} P(|\tilde{\theta} - \theta| > \delta) = 0, \tag{1.24}$$

where δ is an arbitrarily small constant, then $\tilde{\theta}$ is said to be a consistent estimator. That is, if, as the sample size increases, the probability that the absolute difference between the estimator $\tilde{\theta}$ and the parameter θ being greater than some small value δ is 0, then $\tilde{\theta}$ is a consistent estimator of θ. For large sample sizes, a consistent estimator is as good as an unbiased estimator.

So far, I have given properties regarding the estimator relative to some parameter. As an estimator is a function of a random variable, it too has variance or dispersion. The property of *efficiency* introduces this variance in a formal way in order to judge further among competing estimators usually within a class of estimators (e.g., unbiased or consistent estimators). An efficient estimator is one that has achieved the lowest possible variance among all other estimators, and thus has the most precision among all estimators.

For heuristic purposes, recall the three-dimensional log-likelihood surface in Figure 1.6 for a simple regression model. Say we are interested in choosing between two alternative estimators, both of which are consistent estimators. The logic of efficiency tells us to choose the estimator that has the most precision. Graphically, this is equivalent to choosing the estimator that has the steepest climb up to a solution point that is well defined. Take, for example, an extreme case where the surface at the top of the climb is not a point but a plateau. If you could actually climb such a surface, upon reaching the top, everywhere you would look you would see a flat horizontal plane. Imagine yourself, then, being able to move about this plane. Because it is at the top of the surface, the plane represents a solution. However, because it is a plane, anywhere you would stand on it represents an equally valid solution. Because there are an infinite number of coordinates where you could stand, the solution (actually, the solutions) is ill defined, having infinite variance and no efficiency.

As mentioned, that scenario gives an extreme case. Most often we are dealing with estimators with degrees of "roundedness" at the top of the imaginary surface. That estimator with the least amount of roundedness, or with the sharpest descent from the solution, of all estimators is called the most efficient. Again, graphic techniques are not very reliable, and beyond three dimensions they are of little use. We therefore need to use once again the tools afforded us by calculus to assess the efficiency of alternative estimators.

First recall that the first derivative represents the slope of a line tangent to some surface. Second, the second derivative tells us the rate of acceleration of an object from some fixed point. For example, the second derivative is useful in assessing the rate at which an imaginary object would accelerate away from the solution point if left to its own devices. For our plateau example, there would be no acceleration because of the horizontal and flat features of the plateau. The faster the acceleration away from the solution point, the less variance in the solution and the more efficiency it has.

For a parameter vector, what is referred to as the *Fisher information matrix,* after R. A. Fisher, contains the information needed to assess the maximum amount of efficiency that an estimator of the parameter vector may have. The Fisher information matrix for one case out of a total of N cases is given by

$$\mathrm{I}(\boldsymbol{\theta}) = \mathrm{E}[\lambda'(\boldsymbol{\theta})^2] = -\mathrm{E}[\lambda''(\boldsymbol{\theta})], \tag{1.25}$$

where $\lambda'(\boldsymbol{\theta})$ is the first derivative of the log-likelihood with respect to some parameter vector $\boldsymbol{\theta}$, $\lambda''(\boldsymbol{\theta})$ is the corresponding second derivative, and E(.) is the expectation operator over the parameter space for $\boldsymbol{\theta}$.

Now, for an estimator of $\boldsymbol{\theta}$, say $\tilde{\boldsymbol{\theta}}$, the inequality commonly known as the Rao-Cramér inequality tells us that

$$\mathrm{V}(\tilde{\boldsymbol{\theta}}) \geq \frac{[\mathrm{E}'(\tilde{\boldsymbol{\theta}})]^2}{N\mathrm{I}(\boldsymbol{\theta})}, \tag{1.26}$$

where $\mathrm{V}(\tilde{\boldsymbol{\theta}})$ is the variance of the estimator $\tilde{\boldsymbol{\theta}}$ and $\mathrm{E}'(\tilde{\boldsymbol{\theta}})$ is the first derivative of the expected value of $\tilde{\boldsymbol{\theta}}$. This essentially states that the variance for all possible estimators of $\boldsymbol{\theta}$ is bounded by the ratio on the right-hand side of the inequality, and those that achieve that ratio are considered the most efficient estimators for $\boldsymbol{\theta}$. In other words, given a class of unbiased or consistent estimators, the most efficient, or minimum variance, estimator within its class is very desirable in that it has the least amount of dispersion around its expected value and is the most precise estimator of the corresponding parameter.

Maximum likelihood estimators generally have very desirable properties. If a maximum likelihood solution exists, then the maximum likelihood estimate, denoted $\hat{\boldsymbol{\theta}}$, will be both a consistent and, within the class of consistent estimators, a most efficient estimator for $\boldsymbol{\theta}$, given a specified PDF or PF. For all practical purposes, which contain all the cases discussed in this monograph, the maximum likelihood estimator will also be asymptotically unbiased (Stuart & Ord, 1991). That is, as the sample size grows large, the MLE tends toward the properties of an unbiased estimator. Further, if it can be shown that the MLE is unbiased in general, then it will be the minimum variance—that is, most efficient—unbiased estimator. Finally, as I discuss in more detail in Chapter 3, the sampling distribution of the MLE is asymptotically normal (i.e., the sampling distribution of the MLE approaches the normal distribution as the sample size grows large). With large samples, the MLE has very desirable properties.[3] (See note 2 concerning determination of how large is "large enough.")

2. A GENERAL MODELING FRAMEWORK USING MAXIMUM LIKELIHOOD METHODS

The above example showing the equivalence of ML and OLS estimators under certain conditions serves as a launching point for a more general modeling approach employing the principle of maximum likelihood. Only under the assumption that $\boldsymbol{Y} \sim \mathrm{N}(\boldsymbol{X\beta},\sigma^2)$ are the ML and OLS estimators for the model parameters equivalent. If we are satisfied that such an assumption holds, it makes no difference which estimators, ML or OLS, are used. However, if this assumption is questionable, or if we need a more flexible modeling and estimation procedure, then the framework described below becomes useful.

The general modeling strategy discussed here comprises two components: specification of the PDF or PF for the endogenous random variable(s) or dependent variable(s) and specification of structural models linking parameters governing the PDF or PF with exogenous fixed factors or independent variables. This strategy is similar to the generalized linear model (GLM) elaborated in McCullagh and Nelder (1989). The framework given here, however, can handle more complex modeling schemes with more ease than can the GLM. Actually, the GLM is a special case of this strategy. This approach is also very similar to the ML approach advocated by King (1989).

The first component, specification of the PDF or PF, requires consideration of the stochastic properties of the process generating the endogenous random variable, typically denoted the dependent variable in most modeling contexts. The process may result in a discrete or continuous random variable as described above. If we are to model social class, occupational classifications, or similar positions, then we would require a PF for a discrete variable. If, on the other hand, we are to model some distribution of rewards such as wages, then we would require a PDF for a continuous variable.

The range of values from the resulting process must also be considered. For example, the normal distribution assumes the random variable can take on any value on the real number line. The gamma distribution, on the other hand, allows for only nonnegative values. Sometimes we have a process resulting in the truncation of the variable at some minimum or maximum. This would lead us to consider a truncated PDF of the Tobit type (Amemiya, 1985; Maddala, 1983; see also Chapter 5).

In general, for a random variable Y, we should consider the distributional characteristics of Y and the candidate forms for its PDF or PF, here denoted $f(y;\boldsymbol{\theta})$, with $\boldsymbol{\theta}$ being a vector of PDF or PF parameters (e.g., μ and σ^2 in the normal PDF). There are primarily two ways to determine these properties. First, if sufficiently specified, social theory should indicate the nature of these stochastic properties. For example, rational choice theory and the utility maximization principle are sometimes sufficiently rich enough to indicate directly, or to imply indirectly, the proper distributional form of Y (e.g., Coleman, 1990). Similarly, Jasso's (1990) theory of comparison processes or Stryker's (1992) theory of legitimacy processes is sufficiently specified to indicate candidate distributions. Also, most theories of social class lead to a specification in discrete space, and thus imply a corresponding discrete distribution (e.g., Goldthorpe, 1987; Roemer, 1986; Wright, 1985).

Second, if theory is not sufficiently rich to indicate an appropriate PDF or PF, or if it is simply not applicable, and if no prior information is available to determine the stochastic properties of Y, then examination of the realizations of Y, the data values y_i, may be useful in determining such properties. Examination of histograms, frequency distributions, other types of graphs, and univariate statistics can be useful when no theoretical information is available.

Once an appropriate PDF or PF is chosen, we must next specify some function linking the PDF/PF parameter vector $\boldsymbol{\theta}$ to one or more fixed exogenous factors. For $i = 1, \ldots, N$ cases in a sample and $k = 1, \ldots, p$ elements in $\boldsymbol{\theta}$, this specification may be written

$$\theta_{ki} = g_k(\boldsymbol{x}_{ki}), \tag{2.1}$$

where θ_{ki} denotes the value of the kth element in $\boldsymbol{\theta}$ associated with case i, $g_k(.)$ denotes the kth function linking the kth set of factors for case i to the kth element in $\boldsymbol{\theta}$, and where $\boldsymbol{x}_{ki}$ denotes the values of the $1 \times q_k$ vector of fixed factors for the kth PDF/PF parameter and case i. Note that the column dimension of $\boldsymbol{x}_{ki}$ may also change by k, thus the q_k notation.

The form of $g_k(.)$ (e.g., linear, loglinear, or some other more complex function) may be specified either through theory or other prior information as mentioned above for the PDF/PF specifications. However, in determining the form of the function $g_k(.)$, we must take care to consider the range and behavior of the corresponding $\boldsymbol{\theta}$ in the PDF or PF. For example, if we are modeling the probabilities in the multinomial distribution, it is not appropriate to specify a link function such that $g_k(.) > 1$ or $g_k(.) < 0$. An example at this point should prove useful.

The overall model for the normal PDF can be partitioned into two structural links, one for μ and one for σ^2. That is, for the normal PDF, Equation 2.1 can be written as

$$\mu_i = g_1(\boldsymbol{x}_{1i}) \tag{2.2}$$

$$\sigma_i^2 = g_2(\boldsymbol{x}_{2i}). \tag{2.3}$$

Note that $\boldsymbol{x}_1$ is not required to be the same as $\boldsymbol{x}_2$, hence the different subscripts. Similarly, the two functions may also be different, hence the different subscripts there as well.

To relate the normal PDF model to the usual linear regression model, consider a linear function in $\boldsymbol{x}_{1i}$ for $g_1(\boldsymbol{x}_{1i})$ and a loglinear function in $\boldsymbol{x}_{2i}$ for $g_2(\boldsymbol{x}_{2i})$ with $\boldsymbol{x}_{2i}$ consisting of only a constant term for all i. That is, consider the following specifications for Equations 2.2 and 2.3:

$$\mu_i = \boldsymbol{x}_{1i}\boldsymbol{\beta} \tag{2.4}$$

$$\sigma_i^2 = \exp(\gamma), \tag{2.5}$$

with $\boldsymbol{\beta}$ being a column vector of model parameters and γ also being a model parameter. As emphasized above, we take care to specify Equation 2.5 such that $\sigma^2 > 0$. Thus the exponential function, or loglinear specification, is used in Equation 2.5 rather than a linear specification.

Most times we are able to rewrite the link functions in terms of $E(\boldsymbol{Y})$ and $V(\boldsymbol{Y})$. For Equations 2.4 and 2.5 we have the exact same functions written

$$E(Y_i) = \boldsymbol{x}_{1i}\boldsymbol{\beta} \tag{2.6}$$

$$V(Y_i) = \exp(\gamma). \tag{2.7}$$

This model is equivalent to the normal error linear regression model. Further, this specification of the normal PDF model will produce the same estimates for the $\boldsymbol{\beta}$ as in ordinary least squares estimation of the linear regression model. Also note that Equation 2.5 strictly enforces the property of constant error variance given that σ_i^2 depends only on a constant term γ for all i. A natural extension of the normal PDF model is to expand Equation 2.5 to include factors other than the constant term. From this expanded specification, a test for heteroscedasticity may be conducted. Examples of both the homoscedastic and heteroscedastic specifications are given immediately below, along with useful inferential testing procedures.

The Normal PDF Model

The following example using the normal PDF is estimated with a sample of the National Longitudinal Survey of Youth cross-sectional sample (Center for Human Resource Research, 1988). Those included in the sample graduated high school or received equivalent degrees in 1979 or 1980. The data used for the models are primarily from labor market attainments and occupations in 1987 and are given in more detail for each specification used. The total sample size for these normal PDF models is 814.

The normal PDF is one of the most commonly used distributions in model estimation. The normal distribution is appropriate when the endogenous random variable, or some function of it, can take on both positive and negative values. The normal PDF has two parameters and can be written

$$\mathrm{f}(y;\mu,\sigma^2)=\frac{1}{\sqrt{2\pi\sigma^2}}\exp\left[\frac{-(y-\mu)^2}{2\sigma^2}\right] \qquad -\infty<y<+\infty; \qquad (2.8)$$

$$-\infty<\mu<+\infty;\ 0<\sigma^2<+\infty$$

with Y being the endogenous random variable having range on the entire real number line, $\mathrm{E}(Y)=\mu$, and $\mathrm{V}(Y)=\sigma^2$. See Figure 1.1 in Chapter 1 for some shapes that the normal PDF may take.

The log-likelihood for the normal distribution with a sample of $i = 1, \ldots, N$ independently drawn cases may be written as

$$\ln\left[\prod_{i=1}^{N}\mathrm{f}(y;\mu_i,\sigma_i^2)\right]=-\sum_{i=1}^{N}(\ln\sqrt{2\pi\sigma_i^2})-\sum_{i=1}^{N}\frac{1}{2\sigma_i^2}(y_i-\mu_i)^2 . \qquad (2.9)$$

For the general specification of the normal PDF model, we subscript both μ and σ^2 by i to allow for both parameters to vary by i. The Appendix to this monograph gives Gauss code to estimate the normal PDF models described below. Because the Gauss code is sufficiently addressed in the Appendix, it is not described here.

Simple *Z* Tests and Confidence Intervals: The Homoscedastic Normal PDF Model

As was shown in Chapter 1, under certain conditions, OLS estimators and ML estimators for the linear model are the same. To achieve this simple case in the present context, we may use the following link functions for μ and σ^2,

$$\mu_i = \beta_0 + \sum_{j=1}^{p} \beta_j x_{ij} \tag{2.10}$$

$$\sigma_i^2 = \exp(\gamma_0)\,, \tag{2.11}$$

with Equation 2.10 being the usual linear model and γ_0 in Equation 2.11 being a model parameter. Note that the set of x's may contain power terms (squared, cubic, and the like) and interactions as in the usual multiple regression model. Note also that the specification in Equation 2.11 strictly enforces homoscedasticity. Because $0 < \sigma^2 < \infty$, Equation 2.11 is specified as a loglinear, rather than linear, link function. With the link functions for μ and σ^2 given in Equations 2.10 and 2.11, this model is equivalent to the usual linear regression model written

$$y_i = \beta_0 + \sum_{j=1}^{p} \beta_j x_{ij} + \varepsilon_i\,, \tag{2.12}$$

with ε_i being normally distributed, $E(\varepsilon_i) = 0$, and $V(\varepsilon_i) = \sigma^2$. This is equivalent to

$$E(Y_i) = \beta_0 + \sum_{j=1}^{p} \beta_j x_{ij} \tag{2.13}$$

TABLE 2.1

Homoscedastic Normal PDF Model

Y = log of per hour wage			
$N = 814$			
Log-likelihood = −680.690			
Analysis of Entropy-Based Dispersion			
$R = 0.052$			
Source	*Dispersion*	*Test Statistic*	
Model	37.452	chi-square	74.904
Error	680.670	df	3
Total	718.122	*p* value	0.000

Parameter	*Estimate*	*Standard Error*	*z Ratio*
For μ link function			
CONSTANT(β_0)	1.727	0.092	18.772
TENURE(β_1)	0.027	0.014	1.930
SEI(β_2)	0.005	0.001	5.000
WKSNW(β_3)	−0.010	0.003	−3.333
For σ^2 link function			
CONSTANT(γ_0)	−1.165	0.015	−77.667

$$V(Y_i) = \exp(\gamma_0). \tag{2.14}$$

The following variables from the NLSY data are used to estimate the homoscedastic normal PDF model. The dependent variable y_i is given as the natural log of the per hour wage for individual i in 1987. The set of independent variables, the x_j's, consists of (a) the number of weeks on the job divided by 10 (TENURE), (b) the Duncan Socioeconomic Index (SEI), and (c) the number of weeks not employed at a market job in the previous calendar year (WKSNW), 1986 in this case.

Table 2.1 gives the results from the ML estimation of the homoscedastic normal PDF model, which are equivalent in this case to OLS estimates for the β in Equation 2.12. Because maximum likelihood estimation is based on large sample theory (i.e., asymptotic theory), and because the sampling distribution of the MLE is asymptotically normal (see Chapter 3), the standard unit normal distribution is used in testing hypotheses concerning a single parameter. With $\hat{\beta}$ being the MLE for

β and ase($\hat{\beta}$) being an estimate of the asymptotic standard error of $\hat{\beta}$, to test the null hypothesis that β equals some value, say β^*, we may use the following test statistic:

$$z = \frac{\hat{\beta} - \beta^*}{\text{ase}(\hat{\beta})}. \tag{2.15}$$

Under the truth of the null hypothesis, the ratio given in Equation 2.15 will have a standard unit normal distribution. In most cases ase($\hat{\beta}$) will be a by-product of obtaining $\hat{\beta}$ and can be retrieved from the square root of the diagonal of the covariance matrix as described in the second example in Chapter 1.

For example, to assess whether an individual's occupational status has a significant influence on the log of per hour wage, we take the ratio of the estimate for SEI to its estimated asymptotic standard error. Note that, implicitly, in so doing we are setting $\beta^* = 0$. The appropriate ratio gives $z = 0.005/0.001 = 5.00$. As is usual in tests of this type, we then compare the calculated z ratio to some critical value in the standard unit normal distribution. For a two-tailed test and an $\alpha = .05$ level of significance, the critical $z_{\alpha/2} = \pm 1.96$. Because our calculated z is greater than 1.96, and therefore falls in what is commonly called the rejection region, we reject the null hypothesis that $\beta = 0$ and thus reject the null hypothesis that SEI has no influence on the log of per hour wage. The reader should verify that WKSNW is the only other independent variable that has a significant influence on the dependent variable at the .05 level of significance.

Sometimes we are interested in constructing a confidence interval around the point estimate $\hat{\beta}$. This is easily achieved. Let $z_{\alpha/2}$ be the z score corresponding to a $(1 - \alpha) \times 100\%$ confidence interval. The confidence interval is then constructed in the usual manner:

$$\hat{\beta} \pm z_{\alpha/2}\, \text{ase}(\hat{\beta}). \tag{2.16}$$

For example, a 95% confidence interval for the estimate of SEI is given by $0.005 \pm 1.96(0.001) = [0.003, 0.007]$.

Finally, for this model note that $\hat{\gamma} = -1.165$, which gives $\hat{\sigma}^2 = \exp(-1.165) = 0.312$. With $V(Y_i) = \sigma^2$, this serves to emphasize that the variance for this model is constant. That is, the specification of homoscedastic error variance is enforced. Note further that the ML estimate for σ^2 is asymptotically equivalent to the OLS estimator of the error variance.

Likelihood Ratio Tests: The Heteroscedastic Normal PDF Model

Although the *z* test is useful for testing a single parameter, it is less useful when we wish to test a set of parameters. Probably the most common test for multiple parameter situations is the likelihood ratio test. For most ML modeling scenarios, the likelihood ratio test is used in very much the same manner as the general linear *F* test in OLS regression. To see this, suppose we have a set of *p* model parameters, say $\boldsymbol{\beta} = [\beta_1, \ldots, \beta_p]'$. Further, and without loss of generalization, suppose we wish to test whether the first *j* ($j < p$) parameters in $\boldsymbol{\beta}$ are some null value. Most often the null value will be given as zero. We may state this more formally with the null and alternative written

$$H_0: \beta_1 = \ldots = \beta_j = 0$$

$$H_1: \text{some } \beta_1, \ldots, \beta_j \neq 0. \tag{2.17}$$

Test 2.17 is equivalent to testing

$$H_0: \boldsymbol{\beta} = [\beta_{j+1}, \ldots, \beta_p]'$$

$$H_1: \boldsymbol{\beta} = [\beta_1, \ldots, \beta_p]', \tag{2.18}$$

with the parameter vector in the null hypothesis corresponding to a subset of the parameter vector in the alternative. That is, the model corresponding to the null hypothesis is nested within the model corresponding to the alternative.

The guiding principle of the likelihood ratio test is to choose that hypothesis with the highest likelihood of occurrence.[4] That is, given a certain degree of sampling error, choose the hypothesis that maximizes $\Lambda(.)$, the likelihood function defined in Equation 1.6. Let $\hat{\boldsymbol{\beta}}_0$ be the vector of ML estimates under the null hypothesis and $\hat{\boldsymbol{\beta}}_1$ be the vector of ML estimates under the alternative. Define the likelihood ratio as $LR = \Lambda(\hat{\boldsymbol{\beta}}_1)/\Lambda(\hat{\boldsymbol{\beta}}_0)$. If H_0 is true, $2\text{Log}(LR) = 2[\lambda(\hat{\boldsymbol{\beta}}_1) - \lambda(\hat{\boldsymbol{\beta}}_0)]$ will have a chi-square distribution with degrees of freedom equal to the number of parameters set to zero in the null hypothesis. If, however, 2Log(LR) is not chi-square distributed, we conclude in favor of the alternative hypothesis H_1.[5]

For the general case, suppose we have some parameter vector $\boldsymbol{\theta}$ posited to be a member of some parameter space Ω_1. However, we wish to test whether $\boldsymbol{\theta}$ may be a member of a subset of Ω_1, say Ω_0. More succinctly, we wish to test whether $\boldsymbol{\theta} \in \Omega_0$ with $\Omega_0 \subset \Omega_1$ (i.e., that $\boldsymbol{\theta}$ is an element of the restricted parameter space Ω_0, with Ω_0 being a proper subset of Ω_1). We may state this in the traditional hypothesis testing framework as

$$H_0\colon \boldsymbol{\theta} \in \Omega_0$$

$$H_1\colon \boldsymbol{\theta} \in \Omega_1 \text{ with } \Omega_0 \subset \Omega_1. \tag{2.19}$$

The likelihood ratio test for H_0 in the general case is as follows. Let $\hat{\boldsymbol{\theta}}_0$ and $\hat{\boldsymbol{\theta}}_1$ be the maximum likelihood estimates found under models H_0 and H_1, respectively. Further, let $LR = \Lambda(\hat{\boldsymbol{\theta}}_1)/\Lambda(\hat{\boldsymbol{\theta}}_0)$. If H_0 is true, $2\text{Log}(LR) = 2[\lambda(\hat{\boldsymbol{\theta}}_1) - \lambda(\hat{\boldsymbol{\theta}}_0)]$ will have a chi-square distribution with degrees of freedom equal to the number of restrictions imposed on the parameter space Ω_1 giving the subset parameter space Ω_0. If, however, H_0 is not true, then 2Log(LR) will not be chi-square distributed and we conclude in favor of the alternative hypothesis H_1.

To illustrate the likelihood ratio test, I expand the homoscedastic normal PDF model to accommodate factors influencing the variance of the log of per hour wages. Often, because of complex sampling designs or because of the nature of the dependent variable, the assumption of homoscedasticity is just not realistic. For the normal PDF model, introducing heteroscedasticity, or nonconstant variance, into the estimation simply involves extending Equation 2.11 for the variance. That is, we may directly test the source of heteroscedasticity using the ML modeling framework and the likelihood ratio test. This gives the analyst a powerful tool, beyond the usual tools for residual analysis, in controlling for heteroscedasticity. To highlight both this model and the likelihood ratio test, I first consider the use of case weights in the heteroscedastic normal model. This is followed by a further expanded specification for the variance Equation 2.11, which includes the set of independent variables described above for Equation 2.10.

To account for some types of complex sampling designs where case weights are available in the sample, the following link functions become applicable:

$$\mu_i = \beta_0 + \sum_{j=1}^{p} \beta_j x_{ij} \tag{2.20}$$

$$\sigma_i^2 = \exp[\gamma_0 + \gamma_1 \log(z_i)] = \exp(\gamma_0) z_i^{\gamma_1} . \tag{2.21}$$

The link for μ remains the same as in Equation 2.10, whereas the link for σ^2 now includes a constant term plus a term accounting for the weights, z_i. For both Equations 2.20 and 2.21, μ and σ^2 are subscripted by i, allowing each to vary by i. This model may also be written as in Equation 2.12, with $E(\varepsilon_i) = 0$, but now with the heteroscedastic specification $V(\varepsilon_i) = \exp[\gamma_0 + \gamma_1 \log(z_i)]$. This corresponds to

$$E(Y_i) = \beta_0 + \sum_{j=1}^{p} \beta_j x_{ij} \tag{2.22}$$

$$V(Y_i) = \exp[\gamma_0 + \gamma_1 \log(z_i)] . \tag{2.23}$$

An important property of this model should be emphasized. If we fix $\gamma_1 = 1$, rather than estimating γ_1, we obtain results that are asymptotically equivalent to the iterated weighted least squares estimator. However, by estimating γ_1, we are able to test whether $\gamma_1 = 1$ with a two-tailed z test as described in the previous section. The appropriate test statistic is given by the ratio $(\hat{\gamma}_1 - 1)/\text{se}(\hat{\gamma}_1)$, which, under the null hypothesis that $\gamma_1 = 1$, is distributed as a standard unit normal distribution.

With the dependent and the independent variables remaining the same as in the previous example, and with z_i now being included as the case weights, Table 2.2 gives the results of the ML estimation for this heteroscedastic normal PDF model. Again, SEI and WKSNW give significant results at the .05 level with z ratios of 5.00 and –3.33, respectively. However, with a test statistic of $(0.094 - 1)/0.088 = -10.30$ (not shown in Table 2.2), we would reject the hypothesis that $\gamma_1 = 1$, and thus reject the appropriateness of the iterated weighted least squares solution.

The previous test for $\gamma_1 = 1$ tells us only whether or not to reject the hypothesis that $\gamma_1 = 1$. To test for any significant heteroscedasticity as a function of the log of the case weights, we test the hypothesis that $\gamma_1 = 0$ against the alternative that $\gamma_1 \neq 0$. This may be done with either the usual z test or the likelihood ratio test, as with any one-parameter test

TABLE 2.2

Heteroscedastic Normal PDF Model 1

Y = log of per hour wage
N = 814
Log-likelihood = −680.304

Analysis of Entropy-Based Dispersion

R = 0.053

Source	*Dispersion*	*Test Statistic*	
Model	37.818	chi-square	75.636
Error	680.304	df	4
Total	718.122	p value	0.000

Parameter	*Estimate*	*Standard Error*	*z Ratio*
For μ link function			
CONSTANT(β_0)	1.728	0.093	18.581
TENURE(β_1)	0.027	0.014	1.930
SEI(β_2)	0.005	0.001	5.000
WKSNW(β_3)	−0.010	0.003	−3.333
For σ^2 link function			
CONSTANT(γ_0)	−1.165	0.015	−77.667
LogWeights(γ_1)	0.094	0.088	1.068

using an ML framework. Using an $\alpha = 0.05$ level of significance, and with a z ratio of 0.094/0.088 = 1.068, there is no evidence in these data that γ_1 is different from 0.

We can also test the hypothesis that $\gamma_1 = 0$ by means of the likelihood ratio test, because the homoscedastic model is a reduced form of the heteroscedastic model through the restriction that $\gamma_1 = 0$. Under the null hypothesis that $\gamma_1 = 0$, the appropriate test statistic is $2(\lambda_F - \lambda_R)$, where λ_F is the value of the log-likelihood for the full model—the heteroscedastic model—and λ_R is the value of the log-likelihood for the reduced model—the homoscedastic model. If the null hypothesis is true, $2(\lambda_F - \lambda_R)$ should be distributed as a chi-square random variable with degrees of freedom equal to the difference in the number of model parameters estimated, or the number of restrictions on the parameter space, which is one in this case. With $2(\lambda_F - \lambda_R) = 0.772$ on 1 degree of freedom, once again we cannot reject the hypothesis that $\gamma_1 = 0$. And once again we have no evidence to suggest that there exists significant heteroscedasticity as a function of the case weights.

To illustrate the likelihood ratio test further, beyond the somewhat redundant one-parameter case, consider a further expansion of the equation for the variance. Toward this end, consider an extension of Equation 2.21 written

$$\sigma_i^2 = \exp\left[\gamma_0 + \gamma_1 \log(z_i) + \sum_{j=1}^{p} \gamma_{j+1} \log(x_{ij})\right] \tag{2.24}$$

where z_i is once again the case weight for case i and the x_{ij} are the set of independent variables included in Equation 2.13 for $E(Y_i)$. In general, the set of factors in Equation 2.24 need not be the same as those found in Equation 2.13 and may also include power terms (squared, cubic, and the like) and/or interactions as in the usual multiple regression model. This heteroscedastic specification now posits that $E(\varepsilon_i) = 0$ and $V(\varepsilon_i) = \exp[\gamma_0 + \gamma_1 \log(z_i) + \Sigma_{j=1}^{p} \gamma_{j+1} \log(x_{ij})]$. This corresponds to

$$E(Y_i) = \beta_0 + \sum_{j=1}^{p} \beta_j x_{ij} \tag{2.25}$$

$$V(Y_i) = \exp\left[\gamma_0 + \gamma_1 \log(z_i) + \sum_{j=1}^{p} \gamma_{j+1} \log(x_{ij})\right]. \tag{2.26}$$

Table 2.3 gives the results for this heteroscedastic specification. Because this heteroscedastic model is a reduced form of the homoscedastic model given in Equation 2.11, the likelihood ratio test may be employed to test for the joint influence of the variables on the right-hand side of Equation 2.24 on nonconstant variance. More precisely, with the likelihood ratio test we can test

$$H_0: \gamma_1 = \gamma_2 = \gamma_3 = \gamma_4 = 0$$

$$H_1: \text{some } \gamma_1, \ldots, \gamma_4 \neq 0.$$

Note that the constant term, γ_0, must remain in the model to allow σ^2 to be different from one. The value of the appropriate test statistic is $2(680.6895 - 675.0918) = 11.1954$ and, with 4 degrees of freedom, is

TABLE 2.3
Heteroscedastic Normal PDF Model 2

Y = log of per hour wage
$N = 814$
Log-likelihood = −675.092

Analysis of Entropy-Based Dispersion

$R = 0.060$

Source	*Dispersion*	*Test Statistic*	
Model	43.030	chi-square	86.060
Error	675.092	df	7
Total	718.122	p value	0.000

Parameter	*Estimate*	*Standard Error*	*z Ratio*
For μ link function			
CONSTANT(β_0)	1.727	0.076	22.724
TENURE(β_1)	0.025	0.012	2.083
SEI(β_2)	0.005	0.001	5.000
WKSNW(β_3)	−0.009	0.002	−4.500
For σ^2 link function			
CONSTANT(γ_0)	−1.338	0.223	−6.000
LogWeights(γ_1)	0.102	0.091	1.121
LogTENURE(γ_2)	0.346	0.084	4.119
LogSEI(γ_3)	−0.044	0.049	−0.898
LogWKSNW(γ_4)	0.017	0.006	2.833

significant at the 0.05 level. Thus the likelihood ratio test indicates that we should reject the null hypothesis in favor of significant heteroscedasticity as accounted for by the variables given in Equation 2.24. As with the general linear F test for least squares regression models, this type of likelihood ratio test does not tell us precisely which parameter is different from zero, it tells us only that at least one of those tested is different from zero.

Once a likelihood ratio test is used to test a block of variables, and a significant result obtained, it is then appropriate to use the z test for individual parameters to assess which variables are significant. At the $\alpha = 0.05$ level of significance, the z ratios show significant sources of heteroscedasticity in TENURE (0.346/0.084 = 4.119) and in WKSNW (0.017/0.006 = 2.83). These estimates indicate that there is more dispersion of per hour wages for those who have more tenure on the job relative to those who have less tenure. Similarly, those who have more weeks unemployed or out of the labor force in the previous calendar year tend to have a higher dispersion of wages than others.

Not only does this model point out important sources of heteroscedasticity, it also results in a difference in the significance of effects of the independent variables on E(Y). As in the previous specifications, the z ratios of SEI and WKSNW indicate significant effects. However, this heteroscedastic specification also detects a significant effect of TENURE where the previous specifications did not. Though the estimate for TENURE does not change much over the three models, the standard error has decreased enough to give a significant result. Here, the z ratio for TENURE is 0.025/0.012 = 2.083, indicating that those with more tenure on the job do appear to accrue more wages than those with less tenure. This is not an unexpected result, but one that had been masked for this sample in the previous two model specifications.

Wald Tests

Sometimes it is too inconvenient to estimate two models, one for the null and one for the alternative hypothesis, in which to apply the likelihood ratio test just described above. In this case, as well as in other cases, application of the Wald test is useful.

Suppose we have the hypothesis testing situation described in either Equation 2.17 or Equation 2.18 with $\boldsymbol{\beta}^* = [\beta_1, \ldots, \beta_j]'$. Let $\hat{V}(\hat{\boldsymbol{\beta}})$ be an estimate of the covariance matrix as described in Equation 3.5, 3.6, or 3.7 for the full array of elements in $\boldsymbol{\beta}$ from the full model, and let $\hat{V}(\hat{\boldsymbol{\beta}}^*)$ be the $j \times j$ submatrix in $\hat{V}(\hat{\boldsymbol{\beta}})$ corresponding to the j parameters to be tested. Under the null hypothesis described in Equation 2.17 or Equation 2.18, the Wald statistic ω, written

$$\omega = (\hat{\boldsymbol{\beta}}^*)'[\hat{V}(\hat{\boldsymbol{\beta}}^*)]^{-1}(\hat{\boldsymbol{\beta}}^*), \tag{2.27}$$

will be distributed as a chi-square with j degrees of freedom.

For example, the Wald test for the block of variables tested in the previous likelihood ratio test for heteroscedasticity gives $\omega = 26.72$. For this test, and with notation shifted slightly to accommodate the γ notation of the previous section, $\hat{\gamma}^* = [0.102, 0.346, -0.044, 0.017]'$ and

$$\hat{V}(\hat{\gamma}^*) = \begin{bmatrix} 0.008315 & 0.000578 & 0.000027 & 0.000084 \\ 0.000578 & 0.006987 & 0.000172 & 0.000229 \\ 0.000027 & 0.000172 & 0.002389 & 0.000185 \\ 0.000084 & 0.000229 & 0.000185 & 0.000032 \end{bmatrix}.$$

With 4 degrees of freedom, this Wald test indicates a significant result at the 0.05 level of significance. As with the likelihood ratio test, this test also indicates that significant heteroscedasticity exists.

For more general Wald tests where we wish to test $\boldsymbol{\beta}^* = \boldsymbol{\beta}^0$, with $\boldsymbol{\beta}^0$ being a vector of fixed values, we have the test statistic

$$\omega = (\hat{\boldsymbol{\beta}}^* - \boldsymbol{\beta}^0)'[\hat{V}(\hat{\boldsymbol{\beta}}^*)]^{-1}(\hat{\boldsymbol{\beta}}^* - \boldsymbol{\beta}^0). \tag{2.28}$$

Under the null hypothesis that $\boldsymbol{\beta}^* = \boldsymbol{\beta}^0$, ω will be distributed as a chi-square with j degrees of freedom. Equation 2.27 is actually a more restricted form of Equation 2.28 with $\boldsymbol{\beta}^0 = \boldsymbol{0}$.

A General Measure of Association for ML Models

Although hypothesis testing is a very important part of the overall modeling process, so too is measuring the association between the exogenous fixed factor(s) or independent variable(s) in the structural link function(s) of the model and the endogenous random variable(s) or the dependent variable(s). In this section I describe a general measure of association for these models. The measure also gives the amount of dispersion in Y accounted for by the model in the same sense as the R^2 statistic in OLS regression analysis.

Suppose we have a random variable, or dependent variable, of interest, say Y. Further suppose that all the information currently available to the researcher is the PDF or PF of Y and that no structural model is yet posited linking Y with a set of factors. Define the distribution associated with this *marginal information* as f_y, such that MLEs for parameters in f_y are derived only with respect to the data $\boldsymbol{y}$. For example, μ in the normal PDF would be estimated only by $\bar{\boldsymbol{y}}$, the sample mean of $\boldsymbol{y}$.

Now suppose we posit some structural model linking a set of fixed factors or independent variables, say $\boldsymbol{X}$, to one, some, or all parameters found in the PDF or PF of Y. Note that $\boldsymbol{X}$ must include the usual constant term for each structural link function. Define the distribution associated with this *conditional information* about Y given knowledge of $\boldsymbol{X}$ as $f_{y.x}$, where the MLEs are found for model parameters in the usual way.

For a sample of $i = 1, \ldots, N$ cases, let the MLEs for the distributions of the marginal and conditional information for case i be denoted as $\hat{f}_{y(i)}$ and $\hat{f}_{y.x(i)}$, respectively. We can now define components of dispersion derived from Shannon's (1948) entropy measure and used in Haberman (1982). These three components take the form

$$S(Y) = -\sum_{i=1}^{N} \log(\hat{f}_{y(i)}) \tag{2.29}$$

$$S(\boldsymbol{X}) = \sum_{i=1}^{N} \log\left(\frac{\hat{f}_{y.x(i)}}{\hat{f}_{y(i)}}\right) \tag{2.30}$$

$$S(Y \mid \boldsymbol{X}) = \sum_{i=1}^{N} \log(\hat{f}_{y.x(i)}) \tag{2.31}$$

with $S(Y)$ being the total entropy-based dispersion in Y, $S(\boldsymbol{X})$ being the entropy-based dispersion accounted for by the structural model, and $S(Y|\boldsymbol{X})$ being the entropy-based dispersion in Y given $\boldsymbol{X}$, or the error dispersion. When the usual constant term is part of the structural model, it can be verified that the total dispersion is the sum of the dispersion due to the structural model plus the error dispersion. That is, $S(Y) = S(\boldsymbol{X}) + S(Y|\boldsymbol{X})$.

A normed measure of association is derived in a manner similar to the R^2 in OLS regression models. Let R denote the entropy-based measure of association between Y and $\boldsymbol{X}$ with

$$R = 1 - \frac{S(Y \mid \boldsymbol{X})}{S(Y)} = \frac{S(\boldsymbol{X})}{S(Y)}. \tag{2.32}$$

R has a range given by $0 \leq R \leq 1$. When $R = 0$, Y is independent of $\boldsymbol{X}$. When $R = 1$, there is perfect association between Y and $\boldsymbol{X}$. In general, R may be interpreted as follows: Given a specification of f_y, R gives the proportion of the total entropy in Y accounted for by the structural link function(s).

A test for the existence of an association between Y and X using R is readily available. Let ρ be the association in the population between the random variable Y and the fixed factors $\boldsymbol{X}$ given the PDF/PF and link function(s) specifications. To test the null hypothesis that $\rho = 0$ against the alternative that $\rho \neq 0$, we have the test statistic $2S(\boldsymbol{X})$, which, under the truth of the null, will be distributed as a chi-square random variable with degrees of freedom equal to the number of nonredundant parameters estimated in the structural model linking Y with $\boldsymbol{X}$ minus the number of PDF/PF parameters in f_y. If we reject that $2S(\boldsymbol{X})$ is distributed as a chi-square, then we have evidence to suggest that the association between Y and X in the population is different from zero. This is, of course, conditioned on the PDF/PF and link function(s) specifications. This test is the same as the likelihood ratio test for most models where the reduced model contains only the constant term(s). Further, the likelihood ratio test for some model nested within some other model is also a test for a significant reduction in R. This is analogous to the general linear F test in OLS regression models to test for a significant reduction in the R^2 value.

One final point is worth mentioning with respect to this measure of association. Given that the logic behind the marginal and conditional information distributions is independent of the specific form of the PDF or PF, we may use this measure of association to decide which specific PDF or PF best describes the random variable Y and its link with $\boldsymbol{X}$. That is, given a set of candidate PDFs (PFs) to describe Y and a fixed set of factors $\boldsymbol{X}$, we should choose the PDF (PF) that gives the maximum value of R. The PDF or PF that gives the maximum R will correspond to the one in which the set of factors in $\boldsymbol{X}$ is better able to predict values of Y because it is the one that reduces the most amount of uncertainty in Y. In other words, given the same Y and set of factors $\boldsymbol{X}$, the PDF (PF) from a set of candidate PDFs (PFs) that gives the maximum R corresponds to the one that maximizes the amount of information in Y accounted for by $\boldsymbol{X}$. Thus the entropy-based association measure R becomes an important tool for comparing candidate PDFs (PFs) for a given Y and $\boldsymbol{X}$. Unfortunately, no test statistic is currently available to decide more formally which PDF or PF is best. For now, comparison of point estimates of R is the only procedure available.

Returning to our previous examples with the homoscedastic and heteroscedastic normal PDF models, it is useful to illustrate the entropy-based measure of association for these models. For the homoscedastic normal PDF model (see Table 2.1), $R = 0.052$. To test whether ρ, the association between Y and X in the population, is significantly different from 0, we have $2S(X) = 2 \times 37.452 = 74.904$, which, under the null hypothesis that $\rho = 0$, should be distributed as a chi-square random variable with 3 degrees of freedom (equal to the number of parameters estimated for the model, 5, minus the number of PDF parameters, 2). Clearly, with this value of the test statistic we reject $\rho = 0$ in favor of $\rho \neq 0$. Thus we conclude that there is a significant association between the set of independent variables and the dependent variable in this case. More precisely, we interpret R as the proportion of *information,* or *entropy,* in Y accounted for by this specification of the model. That is, this specification of the model between X and Y accounts for 5.2% of the total information or entropy in Y.

Given that the homoscedastic normal PDF model is equivalent to the OLS estimated normal error regression model, it is useful to compare the value of R with the usual R^2 used for OLS models. With the sample variance for y being 0.342, $R^2 = 1 - (0.312/0.342) = 0.088$, which is somewhat similar to the value of R calculated above. Notice the difference in the interpretations, however. R^2 gives the amount of variance in Y accounted for by X. The interpretation of R^2 relies on the sample variance of Y as the base; whereas the interpretation of R relies on the probabilities generated by the underlying PDF as the base. Thus for a given dependent variable and the same set of independent variables, but with a different underlying PDF, the value of R may change. This fact can be usefully exploited in determining which underlying PDF results in the most information gain, or, to rephrase, which underlying PDF maximizes the association between the dependent variable and the set of independent variables.

For the second heteroscedastic normal PDF model (see Table 2.3), $R = 0.06$. In testing $\rho = 0$ for this model, we have $2S(X) = 86.06$ with 7 degrees of freedom, a significant result. Given that the homoscedastic specification is a reduced form of this heteroscedastic specification, we can test the null hypothesis that $\rho_F = \rho_R$, where ρ_F and ρ_R are the associations for the full (heteroscedastic) and reduced (homoscedastic) models, respectively. As mentioned above, this test is exactly the same as that for the corresponding likelihood ratio test between full and reduced models. Recall that there we found the heteroscedastic specification to be preferred to the homoscedastic specification with a significant test statistic value of 11.1954 on 4 degrees of freedom. From this we reject the hypothesis that $\rho_F = \rho_R$. Thus we conclude that there is a significant loss of information in Y that is attributable to X when imposing the restrictions giving the reduced model.

3. AN INTRODUCTION TO BASIC ESTIMATION TECHNIQUES

The Score Vector, Hessian Matrix, and Sampling Distribution of the MLE

As shown above, finding the MLE involves finding derivatives. In this chapter I discuss the role these derivatives play in a more general manner. I first discuss what is commonly called the *scores* or *score vector,* the vector of first derivatives of the log-likelihood $\lambda(\boldsymbol{\theta})$ with respect to $\boldsymbol{\theta}$. Following a discussion of the scores, I discuss the matrix of second derivatives, commonly called the *Hessian matrix.* Finally, I present the sampling distribution of the MLE.

The score vector, $S(\boldsymbol{\theta})$, is defined as the first derivative of $\lambda(\boldsymbol{\theta})$ with respect to $\boldsymbol{\theta}$ and is given by

$$S(\boldsymbol{\theta}) = \frac{\partial \lambda(\boldsymbol{\theta})}{\partial \boldsymbol{\theta}}. \tag{3.1}$$

As was shown in Chapter 1, to find the MLE, $S(\boldsymbol{\theta})$ is set to zero and the resulting equations are solved for each element in $\boldsymbol{\theta}$. In some cases, however, the analytic form of $S(\boldsymbol{\theta})$ may be fairly complex. Even for those who can find analytic derivatives, $\lambda(\boldsymbol{\theta})$ may be sufficiently complex, as in some mixed distributions, that to find the score vector analytically is sometimes too time-consuming. Many times a closed-form analytic solution, such as that given above for $\boldsymbol{\beta}$ when Y is (conditionally) normally distributed, cannot be found, and numerical approximations must be employed. This is both fortunate and unfortunate. Fortunately, numerical approximations are applicable under a wide variety of log-likelihoods, and thus knowledge of analytic derivatives for specific log-likelihoods is not necessary for one to be able to find MLEs. Unfortunately, however, numerical approximations typically lead to estimates that are not as efficient as those found with analytic derivatives, should these exist. Further, using numerical approximations of the score vector typically involves more computational time in finding a solution. Some of the more common numerical approaches for finding $S(\boldsymbol{\theta})$ are discussed below in the section on the iterative process and updating methods.

As we also saw in Chapter 1, the matrix of second derivatives, the Hessian matrix, is important to ML estimation. First, the Hessian matrix is necessary to determine if a solution is a maximum rather than a minimum. If the Hessian matrix is negative definite at the solution, then the solution constitutes a maximum. Second, and of considerable importance from an inferential standpoint, the Hessian matrix defines the covariance matrix for the parameter estimates.

For a parameter vector $\boldsymbol{\theta}$, the Hessian matrix $H(\boldsymbol{\theta})$ is defined as

$$H(\boldsymbol{\theta}) = \frac{\partial^2 \lambda(\boldsymbol{\theta})}{\partial \theta_i \partial \theta_j} . \tag{3.2}$$

At the true maximum, $H(\boldsymbol{\theta})$ will be negative definite. Also at the true maximum, the covariance matrix $V(\boldsymbol{\theta})$ will be positive definite and given by one of the following

$$V(\boldsymbol{\theta}) = \{-E[H(\boldsymbol{\theta})]\}^{-1} \tag{3.3}$$

$$V(\boldsymbol{\theta}) = \{E[S(\boldsymbol{\theta})S(\boldsymbol{\theta})']\}^{-1}, \tag{3.4}$$

with $-E[H(\boldsymbol{\theta})] = E[S(\boldsymbol{\theta})S(\boldsymbol{\theta})'] = I(\boldsymbol{\theta})$, the Fisher information matrix of Equation 1.25. This shows that, at the maximum, the MLE is indeed a most efficient, or minimum variance, estimator, as discussed in Chapter 1.

The covariance matrix of the MLE for $\boldsymbol{\theta}$, $V(\hat{\boldsymbol{\theta}})$, can be obtained from application of either Equation 3.3 or 3.4. The maximum likelihood estimate of $V(\hat{\boldsymbol{\theta}})$, $\hat{V}(\hat{\boldsymbol{\theta}})$, is given by

$$\hat{V}(\hat{\boldsymbol{\theta}}) = [-H(\hat{\boldsymbol{\theta}})]^{-1}. \tag{3.5}$$

For a sample with $i = 1, \ldots, N$ independently drawn cases, consistent estimators for $V(\hat{\boldsymbol{\theta}})$, say $\tilde{V}(\hat{\boldsymbol{\theta}})$, may be obtained by

$$\tilde{V}(\hat{\boldsymbol{\theta}}) = \left[-\sum_{i=1}^{N} H_i(\hat{\boldsymbol{\theta}}) \right]^{-1} \tag{3.6}$$

or by

$$\tilde{V}(\hat{\boldsymbol{\theta}}) = \left[\sum_{i=1}^{N} \mathbf{S}_i(\hat{\boldsymbol{\theta}}) \mathbf{S}_i(\hat{\boldsymbol{\theta}})' \right]^{-1} . \tag{3.7}$$

With the covariance matrix now defined for the MLE in general, we can give the asymptotic distribution of the MLE. Let $\hat{\theta}$ be a scalar MLE for θ and $\sqrt{V(\hat{\theta})}$ be the asymptotic standard error for $\hat{\theta}$. Then as N, the sample size, increases toward infinity, it can be shown that

$$\frac{\hat{\theta} - \theta}{\sqrt{V(\hat{\theta})}} \xrightarrow{D} N(0, 1)\,. \tag{3.8}$$

That is, the ratio given in Equation 3.8 converges in distribution to a standard unit normal distribution. This is an extremely powerful result and is the basis for the z test, as well as the other inference tests, discussed in Chapter 2. Regardless of the PDF or PF used in the estimation procedure and regardless of the form of the link functions used in the model, $\hat{\theta}$ converges in distribution to a normal random variable with mean θ and variance given by Equation 3.3 or 3.4. For various approaches to deriving the asymptotic distribution of the MLE, see Cramer (1986), Amemiya (1985), King (1989), and Stuart and Ord (1991).

The Iterative Process and Updating Methods

Finding the MLE sometimes involves an iterative process. Often we do not have a closed-form solution as with the ML and OLS estimators for the normal-error linear model. However, if a closed-form solution can be found, then no iteration or updating methods are necessary. If, on the other hand, a closed-form solution cannot be found, an iterative process becomes necessary.

To discuss the iterative process, it may be useful to imagine a graph of the log-likelihood surface as given in Figure 1.6. In an iterative procedure, the goal is to try to move efficiently along the log-likelihood surface, getting ever closer to its peak. This procedure may be usefully thought of in three steps. First, imagine yourself starting out on the log-likelihood surface some distance from the maximum. Your starting point on that surface can be given by a corresponding set of coordinates. These coordinates, in turn, represent a set of start values for the vector of parameters you wish to estimate. Second, from your starting coordinates, you require some means by which to move you closer to the peak. This update step corresponds to moving the vector closer to the ML solution. Finally, you need some way to check if you are at the peak, the ML solution. This corresponds to checking the new set of coordinates, or estimates, to assess if a maximum has been achieved. If you determine that a maximum has been achieved, you then quit your search and use that set of estimates as the maximum likelihood solution. If, on the other hand, you determine that a solution has not yet been reached, you then repeat the second and third steps until a solution is obtained. I discuss this process in more detail immediately below.

Obtaining Start Values

A good set of start values can be crucial to the entire iterative process, especially with complex models. All else being equal, a solution will be obtained more quickly when one starts at the base of the incline leading to the maximum than when one starts some distance away from that base. If we have some estimator that gets us close to the ML solution that does not require much work to obtain, then it should be used to generate start values. Sometimes ordinary least squares estimators are consistent for some models. Even if OLS estimators are not consistent, they are often better start values than a vector of zeros. For example, if we posit a normal PDF model with a heteroscedastic error structure, OLS estimates are a good starting point. If we wish to model μ in the gamma PDF, OLS estimates using $\log(Y)$ yield good start values. Though not explicitly discussed, these are used in the examples in Chapter 4. See the Appendix for Gauss code to compute start values for the models used in Chapter 4.

Unfortunately, we sometimes have no idea what a set of good start values might be. In these cases, we may have prior information leading us to believe what the ML solution should look like. Such prior information could come from previous studies similar to the one being conducted, or perhaps some theory may help guide us to a set of appropriate start values. If we have such prior information, it should be used to construct the set of start values.

Often, however, we have no such information. In this case we may do one of two things. First, considering the scale of the variables in the model and the hypothesized scale of the true parameters, we could randomly select a set of start values. On the other hand, we may choose to start with an array of zeros, but only as a last resort. Most times this will allow the iterative process to get off the ground; however, a solution may be many iterations away.

The Update Step and Checking for the Solution

Once start values are obtained, we must decide how to move toward the ML solution. This is typically referred to as the update step. Although an in-depth discussion of various updating methods is beyond the scope of this monograph, I discuss the general approach to updating values of $\boldsymbol{\theta}$ during the iterative process. Cramer (1986), Thisted (1988), and Greene (1993) provide excellent discussions of updating methods.

If we are fortunate enough to have both the analytic first and second derivatives, then we can employ the Newton-Raphson algorithm, also known as quadratic hill climbing. Given a set of start values for $\boldsymbol{\theta}$, say $\boldsymbol{\theta}_0$, we move one step toward the maximum likelihood solution by

$$\boldsymbol{\theta}_1 = \boldsymbol{\theta}_0 - s_0[\mathrm{H}(\boldsymbol{\theta}_0)^{-1}\mathrm{S}(\boldsymbol{\theta}_0)], \tag{3.9}$$

where s_0 is known as the step length, $\mathrm{H}(\boldsymbol{\theta}_0)$ is the Hessian matrix given in Equation 3.2, $\mathrm{S}(\boldsymbol{\theta}_0)$ is the score vector given in Equation 3.1, and $\boldsymbol{\theta}_1$ is the updated vector of parameter values.

In general, for iteration j, we obtain the updated vector of parameter values for iteration $j + 1$ by taking

$$\boldsymbol{\theta}_{j+1} = \boldsymbol{\theta}_j - s_j[\mathrm{H}(\boldsymbol{\theta}_j)^{-1}\mathrm{S}(\boldsymbol{\theta}_j)]. \tag{3.10}$$

The ML solution is obtained when, for all p elements in the parameter vector $\boldsymbol{\theta}$, we have $\max|\theta_{k,j+1} - \theta_{kj}| < \delta_1$, $\lambda_{j+1} - \lambda_j < \delta_2$, $\mathrm{S}(\theta_{k,j+1}) < \delta_3$, or any combination of these three conditions. Here, λ refers to the value of the log-likelihood given in Equation 1.7. Also, δ_1, δ_2, and δ_3 are small values called tolerance levels and are usually set less than 0.01, but whose values should depend on the behavior of the model. Unfortunately, such behavior is usually not known until the model has already been estimated on similar data. Therefore, most analysts tend to use tolerance levels of about 0.01 or less. The smaller the tolerance levels, the more precision in the estimates (with respect to the covariance matrix) and the more likely the true solution will be obtained. In order to move toward a solution, we may update or adjust s_j, $\mathrm{H}(\boldsymbol{\theta}_j)$, $\mathrm{S}(\boldsymbol{\theta}_j)$, or any combination and/or approximation of these at each iteration.

As a rule, a step length should be chosen such that $\lambda(\boldsymbol{\theta})$ at iteration $j + 1$ is a maximum of all possible $\lambda(\boldsymbol{\theta})$ at iteration $j + 1$. Most algorithms default to a value of 1 for s_j. Beyond this simple assignment, there are various methods for adjusting the step length at each iteration. One common method that warrants mention here is the backstep method, which starts with some given value for s_j (in most cases 1) and calculates $\lambda(\boldsymbol{\theta})$ at iteration $j + 1$ using that value. If the $\lambda(\boldsymbol{\theta})$ at $j + 1$ is not larger than that at iteration j, the step length is adjusted using some approximation and another value of s_j is used to recalculate a new $\lambda(\boldsymbol{\theta})$ for iteration $j + 1$. This is done either until $\lambda(\boldsymbol{\theta})$ at $j + 1$ is an improvement over that at j or until it is judged that no improvement for that iteration can be made over the previous iteration. See Dennis and Schnabel (1983) and Berndt, Hall, Hall, and Hausman (1974) for elaboration of this and other methods for adjusting the step length.

For most updating algorithms, we must replace $H(\boldsymbol{\theta}_j)$ of Equation 3.10 with an estimate derived from either Equation 3.3 or 3.4. Using Equation 3.3, we can move toward a solution by taking

$$\boldsymbol{\theta}_{j+1} = \boldsymbol{\theta}_j - s_j\{E[H(\boldsymbol{\theta}_j)]^{-1}S(\boldsymbol{\theta}_j)\} . \qquad (3.11)$$

Using Equation 3.4, we can move toward a solution through

$$\boldsymbol{\theta}_{j+1} = \boldsymbol{\theta}_j - s_j\{E[S(\boldsymbol{\theta}_j)S(\boldsymbol{\theta}_j)']^{-1}S(\boldsymbol{\theta}_j)\} . \qquad (3.12)$$

Because Equation 3.12 involves only the score vector, using 3.12 to find a solution is commonly referred to as the method of scoring (Fisher, 1950).

Often we simply are not fortunate enough to have the analytic derivatives and must employ numerical approximations for $H(\boldsymbol{\theta})$ and/or $S(\boldsymbol{\theta})$ in order to move closer to a solution. Of the various numerical approximations available, three are of particular interest in maximum likelihood estimation. One very useful approach is a modification of the scoring algorithm derived from Equation 3.12. The modified method of scoring developed by Berndt, Hall, Hall, and Hausman (BHHH) (Berndt et al., 1974) incorporates a numerical approximation to the score vector, enabling the researcher who cannot write the vector of first derivatives analytically to use the method of scoring. The BHHH modified method of scoring gives good results when $\boldsymbol{\theta}_j$ is close to the maximum likelihood solution. However, when it is reasonable to suspect that $\boldsymbol{\theta}_j$ is not close to a solution, the BHHH algorithm is less than ideal and will generally take more iterations to find a solution than the following two updating methods.

Two very useful methods for updating values of $\boldsymbol{\theta}_j$ are variations of what are commonly referred to as quasi-Newton updating methods (Thisted, 1988). Broyden, Fletcher, Goldfarb, and Shanno (BFGS) and Davidon, Fletcher, and Powell (DFP) provide useful methods for stepping toward a solution when $\boldsymbol{\theta}_j$ is far from the maximum (Dennis & Schnabel, 1983; Luenberger, 1984). These methods do not require direct calculations of either the second derivatives or the cross-product matrix of the first derivatives in order to move the parameter vector toward a solution. They are typically more efficient than the BHHH algorithm when start values are considerably far from the solution.

Some general rules of thumb for updating values of $\boldsymbol{\theta}_j$ follow. First, when we have the analytic first and second derivatives, it is best to use the Newton-Raphson hill-climbing algorithm from start to finish employing Equation 3.11. When we have only the analytic first derivatives, it is best to use the scoring algorithm from start to finish employing Equation 3.12. When we have neither the first nor the second analytic derivatives, it is best to use the BFGS or DFP algorithms to get close to the solution and then to switch to the BHHH algorithm for the final algorithm(s). Aside from stepping toward the solution at a faster rate when close to the solution, the BHHH algorithm gives a superior approximation to the covariance matrix for the parameters relative to the BFGS and DFP algorithms. The BFGS and DFP algorithms give poor approximations to the covariance matrix at the solution because neither the second derivatives nor the cross-product matrix of the first derivatives is employed in these algorithms. Because of the flexibility required by some models to obtain a maximum, programs such as Gauss that allow the user to change step lengths and/or algorithms during the estimation are particularly useful.

Although these may be regarded as rules of thumb, finding the maximum likelihood solution is sometimes more of an art than a science. If a model fails to converge, any number of parts of the iterative process may be suspect. Poor start values are often to blame. Scaling the independent and/or the dependent variables used in a model so that they have similar range and dispersion very often helps a model to converge more efficiently. Adjustment of the step length is often crucial in ensuring that the algorithm moves smoothly toward a solution. And finally, employing any one of the above updating methods may influence the iterative process substantially.

For newly estimated models, perhaps the best advice is to keep track of the manner in which the log-likelihood moves from iteration to iteration, the values of the score vector at each iteration, and the behavior of the parameter vector at each iteration. If any of these indicate erratic behavior (e.g., getting very large or very small in absolute value with each iteration or oscillating signs from one iteration to the next), then chances are that the model will not converge in a reasonable number of iterations and that the model and/or iterative process will have to be adjusted somehow.

4. FURTHER EMPIRICAL EXAMPLES

The following empirical examples are all estimated with data from the National Longitudinal Survey of Youth cross-sectional sample (Center for Human Resource Research, 1988). Those included in the sample used below graduated high school or received equivalent degrees in 1979 or 1980. The data used for the models are primarily from labor market attainments and occupations in 1987 and are given in more detail for each model below. The total sample size varies by model because of listwise deletion of missing cases; however, for most models the sample size is 814. The specific sample size for each model is given in the corresponding table.

The Gamma PDF Model

A gamma distributed random variable can take on only positive values. In the social sciences this is not much of a limitation, given that many variables of interest, such as wages, status, prestige scores, and most reward structures, take on positive values only. The gamma PDF may be written in a number of different forms, and may contain one or more PDF parameters. The most useful form of the gamma PDF for our purposes contains two parameters and may be written as

$$f(y;\mu,\nu) = \left(\frac{1}{\Gamma(\nu)}\right)\left(\frac{\nu}{\mu}\right)^{\nu} y^{(\nu-1)} \exp\left(\frac{-\nu y}{\mu}\right), \tag{4.1}$$

$$0 \le y < +\infty;\ 0 < \mu < +\infty;\ 0 < \nu < +\infty$$

with $E(Y) = \mu$ (i.e., μ governs the central location of the distribution) and $V(Y) = \mu^2/\nu$ (i.e., μ^2/ν governs the variance of the distribution).

The log-likelihood for the gamma distribution given a sample of $i = 1, \ldots, N$ independently drawn cases may be written

$$\ln\left(\prod_{i=1}^{N} f(y_i;\mu_i,\nu_i)\right) = \tag{4.2}$$

$$\sum_{i=1}^{N}\left\{-\ln\left[\Gamma(\nu_i)\right] + \nu_i \ln\left(\frac{\nu_i}{\mu_i}\right) + (\nu_i - 1)\ln(y_i) - \left(\frac{\nu_i y_i}{\mu_i}\right)\right\}.$$

As in the normal PDF model, we subscript both PDF parameters *i* to allow for both parameters to vary by *i*. The Appendix gives the Gauss code to estimate this gamma PDF model.

The gamma PDF is useful for random variables that take on positive values. This distribution, though popular in the hazard modeling community, has yet to catch on outside of the realm of event-history-style approaches. This is unfortunate, as the gamma distribution is applicable to other social processes/phenomena, such as the attainment of status or market rewards. As we have already seen in Chapter 1 (recall Figures 1.2 and 1.3 also), the gamma distribution is sufficiently flexible to accommodate many distributional shapes. Recall that a gamma distribution provides a reasonable approximation to the wage or income distributions found in the United States. This suggests that the gamma PDF model is well suited for processes involving the attainment of wages, income, or similarly distributed rewards. See Greene (1993) for similar comments.

Given the restrictions on the ranges of μ and ν for the gamma distribution, the general link functions may be written

$$\mu_i = \exp\left(\beta_0 + \sum_{j=1}^{p} \beta_j x_{1ij}\right) \tag{4.3}$$

$$\nu_i = \exp\left(\gamma_0 + \sum_{j=1}^{q} \gamma_j x_{2ij}\right) \tag{4.4}$$

with the β and the γ being model parameters and $\boldsymbol{x}_1$ and $\boldsymbol{x}_2$ being two sets of independent (exogenous) variables. Although $\boldsymbol{x}_1$ and $\boldsymbol{x}_2$ may contain the exact same set of variables, they need not do so. As in the normal PDF model, both sets of $\boldsymbol{x}$'s may include power terms (squared, cubic, or the like) and interactions as in the usual multiple regression model. The gamma PDF model corresponds to

$$\mathrm{E}(Y_i) = \exp\left(\beta_0 + \sum_{j=1}^{p} \beta_j x_{1ij}\right) \tag{4.5}$$

$$V(Y_i) = \exp\left(2\beta_0 - \gamma_0 + 2\sum_{j=1}^{p} \beta_j x_{1ij} - \sum_{j=1}^{q} \gamma_j x_{2ij}\right). \quad (4.6)$$

Thus the model for the central location of the gamma distribution (i.e., that for μ) is given by the loglinear link function in Equation 4.5. Further, the β_j may be interpreted as follows: For every unit change in $\boldsymbol{x}_{1j}$, there will be a β_j change in the natural log of the expected value of $\boldsymbol{Y}$. Note that $\boldsymbol{x}_{1j}$ also influences the variance of $\boldsymbol{Y}$ such that a unit change in $\boldsymbol{x}_{1j}$ results in a $2\beta_j$ change in the natural log of the variance of $\boldsymbol{Y}$. Thus for the gamma PDF model, the set of independent variables given in $\boldsymbol{x}_1$ influences both the mean and the variance of $\boldsymbol{Y}$. This is different from, for example, the homoscedastic normal PDF model, where the set of independent variables given in $\boldsymbol{x}_1$ influences only the mean of the distribution of $\boldsymbol{Y}$.

Constant Coefficient of Variation Model

McCullagh and Nelder (1989) show that for the general linear model, the gamma distribution is useful when we posit a constant coefficient of variation (CV). This specification can be written as a restricted form of the gamma PDF model through a specification of Equation 4.4 with only a constant term. That is, by specifying

$$\nu_i = \exp(\gamma_0) \quad (4.7)$$

we obtain estimates for E(Y) that are based on a constant CV. Specifically, we write the CV as

$$\mathrm{CV} = \frac{\sqrt{V(\boldsymbol{Y})}}{E(\boldsymbol{Y})} = \frac{\sqrt{[\exp(\boldsymbol{x}_1\boldsymbol{\beta})]^2/\exp(\gamma_0)}}{\exp(\boldsymbol{x}_1\boldsymbol{\beta})} = \exp(-0.5\gamma_0). \quad (4.8)$$

Given that CV is often used in assessing the degree of dispersion in wage distributions (or more generally in right-skewed distributions that are anchored at the zero point on the left side of the distribution), this model is a baseline model upon which to build sources of change in CV.

To estimate the gamma PDF model with the NLSY sample discussed above, let y_i be the per hour wage for individual i in 1987 (as opposed to the natural log, which was used in the normal PDF model). Further,

TABLE 4.1
Constant CV Gamma PDF Model

		Y = per hour wage N = 814 Log-likelihood = –3103.286		
		Analysis of Entropy-Based Dispersion		
		R = 0.582		
Source	*Dispersion*	*Test Statistic*		
Model	4328.321	chi-square	8656.642	
Error	3103.286	df	3	
Total	7431.607	p value	0.000	

Parameter	*Estimate*	*Standard Error*	*z Ratio*
For μ link function			
CONSTANT(β_0)	0.743	0.214	3.472
TENURE(β_1)	0.141	0.033	4.273
SEI(β_2)	0.031	0.001	31.000
WKSNW(β_3)	–0.014	0.006	–2.333
For ν link function			
CONSTANT(γ_0)	–0.195	0.060	– 3.250

let the set of $\boldsymbol{x}_1$'s be given as TENURE, SEI, and WKSNW, defined as in the previous example.

Table 4.1 gives the results of the ML estimation for the constant CV model. The z ratios indicate that TENURE, SEI, and WKSNW all have significant influence on wages at the 0.05 level of significance. Specifically, every additional 10 weeks on the job results in an exp(0.141) = 1.151 multiplicative increase in, or about 115% times, the baseline per hour wage. Similarly, every unit increase in the Duncan SEI scale results in an exp(0.031) = 1.031 multiplicative increase in, or about 103% times, the baseline per hour wage. Also, every additional week not working in 1986 results in an exp(–0.014) = 0.986 multiplicative decrease in, or about 99% of, the baseline per hour wage. Finally, to determine the constant CV, we simply take $\exp(-0.5 \times -0.195) = 1.102$.

The value of the entropy-based measure of association, R, may also be calculated for this specification of the gamma PDF model. Toward this end we take $R = 4328.321/7431.591 = 0.582$. This value may be interpreted as follows: Given the gamma PDF, 58.2% of the total entropy-based dispersion (or total information) in per hour wages is accounted for by the model. To test whether this indicates a significant result, we take as our test statistic $2 \times 4328.32 = 8656.64$. At the .05 level of significance with 3 degrees of freedom, we clearly have a significant association between the dependent variable and set of independent variables in the population.

Sources of Variability in CV

Modeling the sources of variability in the coefficient of variation involves expansion of Equation 4.7 to the more general Equation 4.4. One obvious generalization is simply to include all those variables in $\boldsymbol{x}_1$ in the $\boldsymbol{x}_2$ of Equation 4.4. Table 4.2 gives the results for the model with TENURE, SEI, and WKSNW on the right-hand side of both Equations 4.3 and 4.4 with y_i still being per hour wages. To first test the hypothesis that the inclusion of TENURE, SEI, and WKSNW in Equation 4.4 is significant to the model, we may use the likelihood ratio test. The null hypothesis is given as H_0: $\gamma_1 = \gamma_2 = \gamma_3 = 0$ and the alternative is that at least one γ_j ($j = 1, 2, 3$) is not 0. As usual, to test this null with the likelihood ratio test, we take $2(3103.286 - 2907.594) = 391.384$, which, under the null, is distributed as a chi-square random variable on 3 degrees of freedom. Clearly, we reject H_0 in favor of the alternative.

The likelihood ratio test is also a test for a significant change in the entropy-based association measure R. For the nonconstant CV model, $R = 0.609$, a significant increase beyond the R for the constant CV model estimated above. Thus we must conclude that there is significant source of variability in the coefficient of variation, and that this model includes significant association between per hour wages and the set of independent variables, TENURE, SEI, and WKSNW, not accounted for by the constant CV model.

The set of factors influencing the expected value of wages remains about the same as in the constant CV model and gives rise to interpretations similar to those given above. To interpret the sources of variability on the CV, we must use the following generalization of Equation 4.8:

$$\mathrm{CV}_i = \exp\,[-0.5(\gamma_0 + \sum_{j=1}^{q} \gamma_j x_{2ij})]\,. \tag{4.9}$$

Given the −0.5 factor, the signs for the γ indicate a corresponding opposite change in the CV. Thus TENURE and SEI, which give signifi-

TABLE 4.2
Nonconstant CV Gamma PDF Model

Y = per hour wage			
N = 814			
Log-likelihood = −2907.594			
Analysis of Entropy-Based Dispersion			
R = 0.609			
Source	*Dispersion*	*Test Statistic*	
Model	4524.013	chi-square	9048.026
Error	2907.594	df	6
Total	7431.607	p value	0.000

Parameter	*Estimate*	*Standard Error*	*z Ratio*
For μ link function			
CONSTANT(β_0)	1.153	0.076	15.171
TENURE(β_1)	0.120	0.015	8.000
SEI(β_2)	0.022	0.002	11.000
WKSNW(β_3)	−0.007	0.002	−3.500
For ν link function			
CONSTANT(γ_0)	2.879	0.185	15.562
TENURE(γ_1)	−0.239	0.029	8.241
SEI(γ_2)	−0.033	0.002	−16.500
WKSNW(γ_3)	−0.005	0.005	−1.000

cant results through the z ratios at the 0.05 level of significance (−8.241 and −16.500, respectively), indicate that as their values *increase,* the CV also *increases*. Specifically, for every additional 10 weeks at work, the coefficient of variation increases by a factor of $\exp(-0.5 \times -0.239) = 1.127$. For every unit increase in the Duncan SEI, the CV also increases by a factor of $\exp(-0.5 \times -0.033) = 1.017$. Because the z ratio for WKSNW (−1.000) does not indicate a significant result, we must conclude that we have no evidence to suggest that γ_3, the parameter associated with WKSNW, is different from 0.

The Multinomial PF Model

The multinomial distribution function is one of the most useful distributions for a discrete random variable. This distribution is appropriate for a categorical endogenous random variable or variables, and is one of the most common distributions used for modeling categorical data. See Bishop, Fienberg, and Holland (1975), Fienberg (1977), Goodman (1978), Haberman (1978a, 1978b), Amemiya (1985), Clogg and Shockey (1988), Agresti (1990), and Sobel (1993b) for thorough and diverse treatments of the model described below. For a discrete dependent variable Y with J total categories, the product multinomial PF has $J - 1$ nonredundant PF parameters to estimate and can be written

$$F(y; p_j) = \left(\frac{N!}{\prod_{j=1}^{J} n_j!}\right)\left(\prod_{j=1}^{J-1} p_j^{n_j}\right)\left(1 - \sum_{j=1}^{J-1} p_j\right)^{N - \sum_{j=1}^{J-1} n_j}, \tag{4.10}$$

$$0 < p_j < 1, \; n_j > 0, \; N = \sum_{j=1}^{J} n_j$$

where $p_j = P(Y = j)$, n_j is the number of cases found in category j of Y, and where N is the total sample size. For the multinomial PF, $E(Y_j) = Np_j$ and $V(Y_j) = Np_j(1 - p_j)$.

The log-likelihood for the multinomial distribution with a sample of $i = 1, \ldots, n_j$ cases in category j may be written

$$\ln\left(\prod_{i=1}^{N} F(y; p_j)\right) = \sum_{i=1}^{N}\sum_{j=1}^{J-1} D_{ij} \log(p_{ij}) + \sum_{i=1}^{N}\left(1 - \sum_{j=1}^{J-1} D_{ij}\right)\log\left(1 - \sum_{j=1}^{J-1} p_{ij}\right) \tag{4.11}$$

where $p_{ij} = P(D_{ij} = 1)$, with D_{ij} being $J - 1$ sets of indicator variables coded 1 if case i is a member of category j of Y and coded 0 otherwise for $j = 1, \ldots, J - 1$. Note that the factorial term in Equation 4.10 does not appear in the log-likelihood because it does not contain the PF parameters p_j and is thus irrelevant to the estimation. The Appendix gives the commented Gauss code to estimate the multinomial PF with the link function described immediately below.

One of the most useful link functions that gives estimates for the p_{ij} within the allowed range of (0,1) is the logit link function, which can be written

$$p_{ij} = \frac{\exp\left(\beta_{j0} + \sum_{k=1}^{p} \beta_{jk} x_{ik}\right)}{1 + \sum_{s=1}^{J-1} \exp\left(\beta_{s0} + \sum_{k=1}^{p} \beta_{sk} x_{ik}\right)} \qquad j = 1, \ldots, J-1 \tag{4.12}$$

and

$$p_{iJ} = \frac{1}{1 + \sum_{s=1}^{J-1} \exp\left(\beta_{s0} + \sum_{k=1}^{p} \beta_{sk} x_{ik}\right)} \qquad j = J \tag{4.13}$$

where the x_{ik} are a set of p exogenous variables expected to influence p_{ij}, the β_{jk} are model parameters associated with category j of Y and x_{ik}. This specification is equivalent to the generalized logit model discussed in Agresti (1990).

It is important to note that, although the multinomial distribution with the logit link function is probably one of the most common distributions used for modeling categorical data, it is by far not the only one. We could also specify a Poisson distribution with a logit link function, a common candidate. Or we could specify other link functions as long as they adhere to the range for the p_j. See the works mentioned above for alternative specifications.

To estimate this model using the same subset of the NLSY as was used above, let D_j indicate a set of occupations such that D_1 indicates white-collar occupations, D_2 indicates blue-collar or farm occupations, D_3 indicates service occupations, and D_4 indicates those cases with no occupation. D_4 is included for exhaustiveness, an important requirement if the β's are to be consistent and efficient estimators. Let the set of x_k's be given as the number of years of education completed (RED), the number of years of education completed by the respondent's father (FED), an indicator for father's occupation being white-collar (FWC), and an indicator for father's occupation being blue-collar or farm (FBCF).

TABLE 4.3
Entropy Measures and Wald Tests for Multinomial PF Model

Y = occupational groups[a]
N = 928
Log-likelihood = −1036.074

Analysis of Entropy-Based Dispersion

$R = 0.079$

Source	*Dispersion*	*Test Statistic*	
Model	88.333	chi-square	176.666
Error	1036.074	df	12
Total	1124.407	p value	0.000

Wald Tests For Independent Variables

Variable	*Wald Statistic*	*p value*
RED	90.645	0.000
FED	0.533	0.912
FWC	3.290	0.349
FBCF	1.216	0.749

a. See text.

Because there are $J - 1$ sets of estimates for each x_k, some procedure should be used to adjust for the simultaneous inference problem that arises when $J > 2$, as in this case. The Wald test discussed above is useful for first determining if the estimates associated with a given independent variable are jointly significant. If the Wald test indicates a significant result, then we examine each estimate for individual significance with the usual z test. Note that a likelihood ratio test could also be used in place of the Wald test by dropping out each independent variable, one at a time, and estimating p reduced models, one for each independent variable. This approach, however, is a bit cumbersome given that p distinct models must be estimated. The Wald tests, on the other hand, may be conducted from the full model that includes all p independent variables, making it more convenient.

Table 4.3 gives the entropy-based association measure R for this model, along with the appropriate Wald statistics. An $R = 0.079$ indicates that about 8% of the total entropy, or information, available in the vector of occupation categories is accounted for by RED, FED, FWC,

TABLE 4.4
Parameter Estimates for the Multinomial PF Model

Parameter	*Estimate*	*Standard Error*	*z Ratio*
For white-collar link function			
CONSTANT(β_{10})	−4.136	0.844	−4.901
RED(β_{11})	0.348	0.057	6.105
FED(β_{12})	0.007	0.033	0.212
FWC(β_{13})	0.504	0.429	1.175
FBCF(β_{14})	−0.060	0.407	−0.147
For blue-collar/farm link function			
CONSTANT(β_{20})	3.132	1.116	2.807
RED(β_{21})	−0.235	0.082	−2.866
FED(β_{22})	−0.015	0.037	−0.405
FWC(β_{23})	0.141	0.480	0.294
FBCF(β_{24})	−0.028	0.447	−0.063
For service link function			
CONSTANT(β_{30})	−0.936	1.245	−0.752
RED(β_{31})	0.027	0.090	0.300
FED(β_{32})	0.012	0.049	0.245
FWC(β_{33})	−0.355	0.557	−0.637
FBCF(β_{34})	−0.513	0.514	−0.998

and FBCF. To test whether this is a significant result, we take $2 \times 88.333 = 176.666$ on 12 degrees of freedom. At the .05 level of significance, we clearly have a significant result. Thus we have a significant association between Y and the set of independent variables in the population.

The Wald statistics indicate that only RED has a significant influence on the probability of being in one of the occupational categories. Given that only RED is significant at this stage, it would be inappropriate for us to examine the z ratios for FED, FWC, and FBCF. To do so would destroy the safeguard that this procedure gives against a multiple inference inflating the true probability of incorrectly rejecting the null hypothesis. Thus we turn only to the z ratios associated with RED.

Table 4.4 gives estimates for the set of β's. The parameter estimates for this model refer to the influence of an independent variable on the log-odds of being in the associated category as opposed to being in the Jth category, sometimes called the reference category (see, e.g., Agresti, 1990). The effect of RED on the odds of being in a white-collar occupation as opposed to not having an occupation is significant with a z ratio of 6.000. Specifically, each year increase in RED leads to a

$\hat{\beta}_{11} = 0.348$ increase in the log-odds of being in a white-collar occupation as opposed to not having an occupation. Similarly, the effect of RED on the odds of being in a blue-collar/farm occupation as opposed to having no occupation is also significant with a *z* ratio of −2.866. Thus each year increase in RED leads to a $\hat{\beta}_{21} = -0.235$ decrease in the log-odds of being in a blue-collar/farm occupation as opposed to not having an occupation. Finally, because the *z* ratio for the effect of RED on being in a service occupation is not significant, we conclude that there is no influence of RED on the corresponding log-odds. Elaboration of these and other transformations of the model parameters will not be given here, because much work has been dedicated to interpretation of functions of the model parameters (see, e.g., Alba, 1988; Long, 1984, 1987).

The Bivariate Normal PDF Model

The bivariate normal PDF is useful when we have two endogenous/dependent variables with reciprocal effects. The bivariate normal PDF has five parameters and can be written

$$f(y_1, y_2; \mu_1, \mu_2, \sigma_1, \sigma_2, \rho) = \tag{4.14}$$

$$\frac{1}{\sqrt{2\pi\sigma_1\sigma_2(1-\rho^2)}}\exp\left\{-\frac{1}{2(1-\rho^2)}\left[\left(\frac{y_1-\mu_1}{\sigma_1}\right)^2 - \rho\left(\frac{y_1-\mu_1}{\sigma_1}\right)\left(\frac{y_2-\mu_2}{\sigma_2}\right) + \left(\frac{y_2-\mu_2}{\sigma_2}\right)^2\right]\right\}$$

$$-\infty < y_1 < +\infty,\ -\infty < y_2 < +\infty,\ -\infty < \mu_1 < +\infty,\ -\infty < \mu_2 < +\infty,$$
$$0 < \sigma_1 < +\infty,\ 0 < \sigma_2 < +\infty,\ -1 < \rho < 1$$

where y_1 and y_2 are the two endogenous random variables of interest, $E(Y_1) = \mu_1$, $E(Y_2) = \mu_2$, $V(Y_1) = \sigma_1^2$, $V(Y_2) = \sigma_2^2$, and $V(Y_1,Y_2)/\sqrt{V(Y_1)V(Y_2)} = \rho$, the correlation between Y_1 and Y_2.

Given that interest often lies in the expected value of one endogenous variable given values of the other, the conditional expectations of one given the other are of interest. These may be written as

$$E(Y_1 \mid y_2) = \mu_1 - (\sigma_1/\sigma_2)\rho\mu_2 + (\sigma_1/\sigma_2)\rho y_2 \tag{4.15}$$

$$E(Y_2 \mid y_1) = \mu_2 - (\sigma_2/\sigma_1)\rho\mu_1 + (\sigma_2/\sigma_1)\rho y_1. \tag{4.16}$$

With these conditional expectations, $(\sigma_1/\sigma_2)\rho$ may be interpreted as the effect of y_2 on y_1 *controlling for* the exogenous factors included in the link functions for μ_1, μ_2, σ_1^2, σ_2^2, and ρ. Similarly, $(\sigma_2/\sigma_1)\rho$ may be interpreted as the effect of y_1 on y_2 *controlling for* the exogenous factors included in the link functions for μ_1, μ_2, σ_1^2, σ_2^2, and ρ.

The log-likelihood for the bivariate normal distribution with a sample of $i = 1, \ldots, N$ independently drawn cases may be written as

$$\log\left[\prod_{i=1}^{N} \mathrm{f}(y_1, y_2; \mu_1, \mu_2, \sigma_1, \sigma_2, \rho)\right] = \tag{4.17}$$

$$\sum_{i=1}^{N}\left\{-\frac{1}{2}\log\left[2\pi\sigma_{1i}\sigma_{2i}(1-\rho_i^2)\right) - \frac{1}{2(1-\rho^2)}\left[\left(\frac{y_{1i}-\mu_{1i}}{\sigma_{1i}}\right)^2 - \rho_i\left(\frac{y_{1i}-\mu_{1i}}{\sigma_{1i}}\right)\left(\frac{y_{2i}-\mu_{2i}}{\sigma_{2i}}\right) + \left(\frac{y_{2i}-\mu_{2i}}{\sigma_{2i}}\right)^2\right]\right\}.$$

The Appendix gives Gauss code to estimate the bivariate normal PDF model.

Appropriate link functions for μ_1, μ_2, σ_1^2, and σ_2^2 are the same as those for the univariate normal distribution given above. A link function for ρ, however, must ensure that $-1 < \rho < 1$. Thus the following set of link functions are appropriate for the bivariate normal,

$$\mu_{ki} = \beta_{k0} + \sum_{j=1}^{p_k} \beta_{kj} x_{kij}, \qquad k = 1, 2 \tag{4.18}$$

$$\sigma_{ki}^2 = \exp\left(\gamma_{k0} + \sum_{j=1}^{q_k} \gamma_{kj} w_{kij}\right), \qquad k = 1, 2 \tag{4.19}$$

$$\rho_i = \frac{\exp\left(\delta_0 + \sum_{j=1}^{r} \delta_j z_{ij}\right) - 1}{\exp\left(\delta_0 + \sum_{j=1}^{r} \delta_j z_{ij}\right) + 1} \tag{4.20}$$

where x_{kij} are the two sets of exogenous factors influencing $E(Y_k)$, $k = 1, 2$, with β_{kj} being the model parameters. Similarly, w_{kij} are the sets of exogenous factors influencing $V(Y_k)$, $k = 1, 2$, with the γ_{kj} being the model parameters. Finally, z_{ij} is a set of exogenous factors influencing the correlation between Y_1 and Y_2, with the δ_j being a set of model parameters. Note that the Y_k are not included in the x_{kij}, w_{kij}, or z_{ij} for identification purposes.

We retrieve the effects of the Y_k on one another through Equations 4.15 and 4.16. These link functions correspond to

$$E(Y_k) = \beta_{k0} + \sum_{j=1}^{p_k} \beta_{kj} x_{kij}, \qquad k = 1, 2 \tag{4.21}$$

$$E(Y_1 \mid y_2) = \beta_{10} + \sum_{j=1}^{p_1} \beta_{1j} x_{1ij} + \left(\frac{\sigma_{1i}}{\sigma_{2i}} \rho_i\right) y_{2i} - \left(\frac{\sigma_{1i}}{\sigma_{2i}} \rho_i\right) \beta_{20} - \left(\frac{\sigma_{1i}}{\sigma_{2i}} \rho_i\right) \sum_{j=1}^{p_2} \beta_{2j} x_{2ij} \tag{4.22}$$

$$E(Y_2 \mid y_1) = \beta_{20} + \sum_{j=1}^{p_2} \beta_{2j} x_{2ij} + \left(\frac{\sigma_{2i}}{\sigma_{1i}} \rho_i\right) y_{1i} - \left(\frac{\sigma_{2i}}{\sigma_{1i}} \rho_i\right) \beta_{10} - \left(\frac{\sigma_{2i}}{\sigma_{1i}} \rho_i\right) \sum_{j=1}^{p_1} \beta_{1j} x_{1ij} \tag{4.23}$$

with variances corresponding to Equation 4.19 and the correlation corresponding to Equation 4.20. If some of the exogenous factors in $\boldsymbol{x}_1$ are also in $\boldsymbol{x}_2$, then we may compare the *marginal* effects of, say, $\boldsymbol{x}_1$ on y_1 as given by Equation 4.21 with the *conditional* effects of $\boldsymbol{x}_1$ on y_1 given y_2 as in Equation 4.22. Specifically, the conditional effect of the jth variable found in both $\boldsymbol{x}_1$ and $\boldsymbol{x}_2$ on y_1 is given by

$$\beta_{1j}^* = \beta_{1j} - (\sigma_1/\sigma_2)\rho\beta_{2j} . \tag{4.24}$$

Similarly, the conditional effect of the jth variable found in both $\boldsymbol{x}_1$ and $\boldsymbol{x}_2$ on y_2 is given by

$$\beta^*_{2j} = \beta_{2j} - (\sigma_2/\sigma_1)\rho\beta_{1j} \,. \tag{4.25}$$

From a comparison of the conditional effects calculated in Equations 4.24 and 4.25 with the respective marginal effects, we may determine the amount of influence the inclusion of, say, y_2 has on $\boldsymbol{x}_j$'s effect on y_1. That is, a comparison of β^*_{1j} with β_{1j} will give the influence of $\boldsymbol{x}_j$ on y_1 with and without the effect of y_2 on y_1, respectively. This holds in a similar way for the influence on y_2 with and without the effect of y_1 on y_2. A test statistic is not currently available for such a comparison in this context, so noting the difference between β^*_{1j} and β_{1j} will have to suffice.[6] However, we can note that as $|\rho|$ increases, so too will the difference. For $\rho = 0$, no difference between the marginal and conditional effects will be found and thus $\beta^*_{1j} = \beta_{1j}$ and $\beta^*_{2j} = \beta_{2j}$. Unfortunately, however, if $\rho \neq 0$, then we cannot infer that $\beta^*_{1j} \neq \beta_{1j}$ and/or $\beta^*_{2j} \neq \beta_{2j}$, because β_{2j} and β_{1j} enter into Equations 4.24 and 4.25, respectively, in a manner similar to ρ.

Of similar importance to the bivariate normal model is whether or not Y_1 is influenced by Y_2, or vice versa. Note that this model is not capable of determining any causal connection between Y_1 and Y_2; other conditions must hold for a causal relationship to hold (see, e.g., Sobel, 1993a). However, if an empirical association is not present, then we have tentative evidence to suggest that Y_1 does not cause Y_2, and vice versa, for a specified model and set of data. Thus a test of the association is important.

Given that $\sigma_1 > 0$ and $\sigma_2 > 0$, a test of whether ρ is significantly different from zero constitutes a test of whether Y_1 and Y_2 are associated, controlling for the set of exogenous factors in the system of equations. Given Equation 4.20 as the link function for ρ, this test is equivalent to testing whether or not the set of δ's are jointly significantly different from zero. This test could be conducted with either the likelihood ratio test or the Wald test discussed above.

In the simpler case of constant correlation, we may rewrite Equation 4.20 as

$$\rho_i = \frac{\exp(\delta_0) - 1}{\exp(\delta_0) + 1} \,. \tag{4.26}$$

Thus the test for H_0: $\delta_0 = 0$ constitutes the test for association between Y_1 and Y_2. For this test, the z ratio $\hat{\delta}_0/\text{ase}(\hat{\delta}_0)$ is distributed as a standard unit normal under H_0. If the test indicates an insignificant result, then Y_1 and Y_2 are not associated with one another, controlling for the set of exogenous factors, and thus the exogenous effects on Y_1 and Y_2 may be estimated with two univariate normal PDF models. If, on the other hand, the test indicates a significant result, then the estimation of the exogenous effects on Y_1 and Y_2 with separate univariate normal PDF models would produce inconsistent and inefficient estimates for the β and γ.

It is currently extremely rare to model the variances and the correlation along with the expected values. There is little social theory at this point that lends itself to consideration of the complex modeling of Equations 4.18, 4.19, and 4.20 simultaneously. However, when nonconstant variance is expected, then models for Equation 4.19 based on the heteroscedastic normal model discussed above are appropriate. Further, if the analyst suspects a bivariate relationship with nonconstant correlation, then inclusion of exogenous factors influencing the correlation should be included in Equation 4.20. For our example here, however, we shall examine a simple model with exogenous factors influencing only $E(Y_k)$ with constant variance and correlation.

The subset of the NLSY data used above will also be used for the example here. The two endogenous variables, Y_1 and Y_2, are the Duncan socioeconomic index (SEI) and the log of per hour wages (LNPHW), respectively. The set of x's is the same for both equations (note that this need not be the case) and is given by TENURE, RED, and WKSNW, described above. Both constant variance and constant correlation are specified. That is, only the γ_0 and δ_0 are estimated.

Table 4.5 gives results (the marginal effects) for the ML estimation of the bivariate normal PDF model with the exogenous factors described above. With the test statistic for the entropy-based association given by $2 \times 122.795 = 245.59$ on 6 degrees of freedom, we have a significant association of $R = 0.028$. Given the z ratios for the exogenous factors, only RED has a significant effect on SEI. On the other hand, all three exogenous factors have a significant influence on LNPHW. As interpretations are similar to those for the normal PDF model for LNPHW, and those regarding SEI are straightforward, I leave these to the reader.

Given a significant z ratio for $\hat{\delta}_0$, $\hat{\delta}_0/\text{ase}(\hat{\delta}_0) = 2.89$, we may conclude that $\rho \neq 0$ and that a significant positive association exists between SEI and LNPHW with $\hat{\rho} = 0.117$ from Equation 4.26. Specifically, the effect of LNPHW on SEI is given by $(\hat{\sigma}_1/\hat{\sigma}_2)\hat{\rho} = 4.168$, with $\hat{\sigma}_1 = 19.806$ being

TABLE 4.5
Bivariate Normal PDF Model

Y_1 = Duncan SEI score
Y_2 = log of per hour wage
$N = 814$
Log-likelihood = –4256.784

Analysis of Entropy-Based Dispersion

$R = 0.028$

Source	*Dispersion*	*Test Statistic*	
Model	122.795	chi-square	245.590
Error	4256.784	df	6
Total	4379.579	p value	0.000

Parameter	*Estimate*	*Standard Error*	*z Ratio*
For μ_1 link function (SEI)			
CONSTANT(β_{10})	–33.646	6.550	– 5.137
TENURE(β_{11})	0.801	0.410	1.954
RED(β_{12})	5.473	0.444	12.327
WKSNW(β_{13})	0.020	0.078	0.256
For μ_2 link function (LNPHW)			
CONSTANT(β_{20})	0.972	0.205	4.741
TENURE(β_{21})	0.035	0.014	2.500
RED(β_{22}) 0.070	0.013	5.385	
WKSNW(β_{23})	–0.010	0.003	– 3.333
For σ_1^2 link function (SEI)			
CONSTANT(γ_{10})	5.972	0.067	89.134
For σ_2^2 link function (LNPHW)			
CONSTANT(γ_{20})	–1.175	0.013	–90.385
For ρ link function			
CONSTANT(δ_0)	0.234	0.081	2.889

the standard error for the SEI equation and $\hat{\sigma}_2 = 0.556$ being the standard error for the LNPHW equation. Similarly, the effect of SEI on LNPHW is given by $(\hat{\sigma}_2/\hat{\sigma}_1)\hat{\rho} = 0.003$. These effects are interpretable as are slopes in the usual regression model.

As $\rho \neq 0$, it is also useful to compare the marginal effects of the exogenous factors with the conditional effects of Equations 4.24 and 4.25. There are at least two very basic reasons to conduct the comparison, one statistical and one substantive. First, the difference between

TABLE 4.6
Conditional Effects for the Bivariate Normal PDF Model

Y_1 = Duncan SEI score
Y_2 = log of per hour wage

Parameter	*Conditional Effects* *Effect on SEI*	*Effect on LNPHW*
TENURE	0.655	0.033
RED	5.181	0.054
WKSNW	0.062	−0.010
SEI	—	0.003
LNPHW	4.168	—

the marginal and conditional effects indicates the amount of inconsistency in the estimate had two univariate models been estimated. Second, it is important substantively to determine the amount of influence that an exogenous factor has on, say, y_1 that is attributable to y_2. This second reason is not unlike comparing the difference between direct and indirect effects in the traditional path analysis.

Conditional effects are given in Table 4.6. The inclusion of the effect of LNPHW on SEI diminishes the marginal effects of RED and TENURE with conditional estimates of 5.181 and 0.655, respectively. On the other hand, the inclusion of LNPHW has the effect of increasing the influence of WKSNW on SEI with a conditional estimate of 0.062. The inclusion of the SEI effect on LNPHW increases the effects of RED and TENURE, with conditional estimates of 0.054 and 0.033, respectively, but has no influence on the effect of WKSNW. Again, these comparisons should be made with caution; currently we have no test statistic to ascertain if the difference observed is beyond that expected by chance.

5. ADDITIONAL LIKELIHOODS

In this chapter I provide two additional models that the reader may find useful—one for the truncated normal distribution and one for the lognormal distribution. For each model I provide the PDF, the log-likelihood, and appropriate structural link functions for the PDF parameters. For a more extensive treatment of ML estimation using PDFs or PFs not found in this monograph, or for the use of ML estimation for models not discussed herein, see King (1989), Cramer (1986), Amemiya (1985), Maddala (1983), and works cited therein. Examples of ML methods discussed in these works that are not given here include those for some discrete data models, time-series models, duration and event-history models, mixed distribution models (e.g., endogenous switching models, sample selection models, and Tobit-type models), and multiple endogenous variables models (e.g., multivariate normal models).

The Truncated Normal PDF Model

The truncated normal is an appropriate PDF for cases where the range of the dependent variable Y is truncated in some manner. Most often, we will encounter a situation where the range is truncated at the lower end of the distribution, at the upper end, or both. These are the cases provided here. For a detailed statistical treatment of the truncated normal distribution, see Schneider (1986). For a discussion of the use of the truncated normal and related distributions, see Maddala (1983) and Amemiya (1985).

Sometimes in research we encounter lower truncation of the range of Y below some value y_L. For example, say we wish to include in the analysis only those individuals with an income, market wage, or some other reward above y_L. For an observation i, the PDF is a conditional PDF, $f(y_i \mid y_L \leq y_i)$, and, assuming normality, may be written

$$f(y_i \mid y_L \leq y_i) = \frac{\dfrac{1}{\sqrt{2\pi\sigma_i^2}} \exp\left[\dfrac{-(y_i - \mu_i)^2}{2\sigma_i^2}\right]}{\displaystyle\int_{y_L}^{+\infty} \dfrac{1}{\sqrt{2\pi\sigma_i^2}} \exp\left[\dfrac{-(t_i - \mu_i)^2}{2\sigma_i^2}\right] dt_i}, \tag{5.1}$$

$$y_L \leq y < +\infty, \quad -\infty < \mu < +\infty, \quad 0 < \sigma^2 < +\infty$$

Letting $\phi(.)$ and $\Phi(.)$ be the PDF and cumulative distribution function for the standard unit normal distribution, the log-likelihood for Equation 5.1 is given by

$$\lambda(\mu, \sigma^2) = \sum_{i=1}^{N} \log\left[\sigma_i^{-1}\phi\left(\frac{y_i - \mu_i}{\sigma_i}\right)\right] - \sum_{i=1}^{N} \log\left[1 - \Phi\left(\frac{y_L - \mu_i}{\sigma_i}\right)\right]. \tag{5.2}$$

The structural links for this model are the same as those for the normal PDF model:

$$\mu_i = \beta_0 + \sum_{j=1}^{p} \beta_j x_{1ij} \tag{5.3}$$

$$\sigma_i^2 = \exp\left(\gamma_0 + \sum_{j=1}^{q} \gamma_j x_{2ij}\right) \tag{5.4}$$

where $\boldsymbol{x}_1$ and $\boldsymbol{x}_2$ are fixed exogenous factors and the β and γ are model parameters. This model corresponds to a model for $E(Y)$ written

$$E(Y_i) = \beta_0 + \sum_{j=1}^{p} \beta_j x_{1ij} + \sigma_i \left\{ \frac{\phi[(y_L - \mu_i)/\sigma_i]}{1 - \Phi[(y_L - \mu_i)/\sigma_i]} \right\} \tag{5.5}$$

where μ_i and σ_i are as given in Equations 5.3 and 5.4, respectively. The term associated with σ_i in Equation 5.5 may be regarded as an adjustment for the truncation. This term can have a considerable influence on the estimation of the β. If we do observe truncation, and the log-likelihood in Equation 5.2 is not used and the normal PDF model is used instead, then the β will not be consistently or efficiently estimated.

Other times we may encounter a situation with upper truncation of the range of Y above some value y_U. For example, studies on poverty may include only those individuals below some specified income level y_U. For an observation i, this upper-truncated PDF is also a conditional PDF, $f(y_i \mid y_U \geq y_i)$, and, assuming normality, may be written

$$f(y_i \mid y_U \geq y_i) = \frac{\dfrac{1}{\sqrt{2\pi\sigma_i^2}} \exp\left[\dfrac{-(y_i - \mu_i)^2}{2\sigma_i^2}\right]}{\displaystyle\int_{-\infty}^{y_U} \frac{1}{\sqrt{2\pi\sigma_i^2}} \exp\left[\frac{-(t_i - \mu_i)^2}{2\sigma_i^2}\right] dt_i}, \tag{5.6}$$

$$-\infty < y \leq y_U, \; -\infty < \mu < +\infty, \; 0 < \sigma^2 < +\infty$$

This has a corresponding log-likelihood written

$$\lambda(\mu, \sigma^2) = \sum_{i=1}^{N} \log\left[\sigma_i^{-1}\phi\left(\frac{y_i - \mu_i}{\sigma_i}\right)\right] - \sum_{i=1}^{N} \log\left[\Phi\left(\frac{y_U - \mu_i}{\sigma_i}\right)\right]. \tag{5.7}$$

The structural links are exactly the same as those given in Equations 5.3 and 5.4, with a corresponding model in E(Y) written

$$E(Y_i) = \beta_0 + \sum_{j=1}^{p} \beta_j x_{1ij} + \sigma_i\left\{\frac{\phi[(y_U - \mu_i)/\sigma_i]}{\Phi[(y_U - \mu_i)/\sigma_i]}\right\}. \tag{5.8}$$

Again, the last term in Equation 5.8 may be regarded as an adjustment for the upper truncation. The comments given for Equation 5.5 apply here also.

Finally, we may encounter both upper and lower truncation. For example, in poverty studies, we may indeed observe only those cases below some y_U. However, some theories of income attainment also indicate that the income level of 0 should be considered a truncation point rather than the true lower bound (e.g., Maddala, 1983). In such a case we have double truncation with y_U dependent on the specific study and $y_L = 0$. In general, with y_L taking on some value such that $y_L < y_U$, this conditional PDF may be written as

$$f(y_i \mid y_L \le y_i \le y_U) = \frac{\frac{1}{\sqrt{2\pi\sigma_i^2}} \exp\left[\frac{-(y_i - \mu_i)^2}{2\sigma_i^2}\right]}{\int_{y_L}^{y_U} \frac{1}{\sqrt{2\pi\sigma_i^2}} \exp\left[\frac{-(t_i - \mu_i)^2}{2\sigma_i^2}\right] dt_i}, \tag{5.9}$$

$$y_L \le y_i \le y_U, \quad -\infty < \mu < +\infty, \quad 0 < \sigma^2 < +\infty .$$

This doubly truncated PDF has a corresponding log-likelihood written

$$\lambda(\mu, \sigma^2) = \sum_{i=1}^{N} \log\left[\sigma_i^{-1}\phi\left(\frac{y_i - \mu_i}{\sigma_i}\right)\right] \tag{5.10}$$

$$- \sum_{i=1}^{N} \log\left[\Phi\left(\frac{y_U - \mu_i}{\sigma_i}\right) - \Phi\left(\frac{y_L - \mu_i}{\sigma_i}\right)\right].$$

Again, the structural links are exactly the same as those given in Equations 5.3 and 5.4, with a corresponding model in E(Y) written

$$E(Y_i) = \beta_0 + \sum_{j=1}^{p} \beta_j x_{1ij} \tag{5.11}$$

$$+ \sigma_i \left\{ \frac{\phi[(y_L - \mu_i)/\sigma_i]}{1 - \Phi[(y_L - \mu_i)/\sigma_i]} - \frac{\phi[(y_U - \mu_i)/\sigma_i]}{\Phi[(y_U - \mu_i)/\sigma_i]} \right\}.$$

As noted above, the last term in Equation 5.11 may be regarded as an adjustment for the upper and lower truncations, and the comments given for Equation 5.5 apply here as well.

The Log-Normal PDF Model

The log-normal PDF model can be considered an alternative to the gamma PDF model. For some nonzero positive-valued random variable Y, if log(Y) can be considered normally distributed conditional on a set of exogenous fixed factors, then the log-normal PDF model becomes appropriate. Thus, for models of market rewards such as wages, a researcher may wish to use the log-normal PDF rather than the gamma PDF, or rather than the normal PDF using log(Y).

The PDF for the log-normal may be written as

$$f(y_i; \mu_i, \sigma_i^2) = \frac{1}{y_i \sqrt{2\pi\sigma_i^2}} \exp \left\{ \frac{-[\log(y_i) - \mu_i]^2}{2\sigma_i^2} \right\}, \tag{5.12}$$

$$0 < y_i < +\infty, \quad -\infty < \mu < +\infty, \quad 0 < \sigma^2 < +\infty$$

with a corresponding log-likelihood written

$$\lambda(\mu, \sigma^2) = \sum_{i=1}^{N} \left\{ -\log(y_i) - \frac{1}{2} \log(2\pi\sigma_i^2) - \frac{1}{2\sigma_i^2} [\log(y_i) - \mu_i]^2 \right\}. \tag{5.13}$$

Appropriate link functions are exactly the same as those for the normal PDF model,

$$\mu_i = \beta_0 + \sum_{j=1}^{p} \beta_j x_{1ij} \tag{5.14}$$

$$\sigma_i^2 = \exp\left(\gamma_0 + \sum_{j=1}^{q} \gamma_j x_{2ij}\right) \tag{5.15}$$

where the $\boldsymbol{x}_1$ and $\boldsymbol{x}_2$ are fixed exogenous factors and the β and γ are model parameters.

Unlike the normal PDF model, however, the models written in terms of E(Y) and V(Y) are

$$\mathrm{E}(Y_i) = \exp\left[\beta_0 + \sum_{j=1}^{p} \beta_j x_{1ij} - 0.5\exp\left(\gamma_0 + \sum_{j=1}^{q} \gamma_j x_{2ij}\right)\right] \tag{5.16}$$

$$\mathrm{V}(Y_i) = \exp\left[\exp\left(\gamma_0 + \sum_{j=1}^{q} \gamma_j x_{2ij}\right)\right] \tag{5.17}$$

$$\times \left\{\exp\left[\exp\left(\gamma_0 + \sum_{j=1}^{q} \gamma_j x_{2ij}\right)\right] - 1\right\}\left\{\exp\left[2\left(\beta_0 + \sum_{j=1}^{p} \beta_j x_{1ij}\right)\right]\right\}$$

Although these are complex forms in the original Y, in the log(Y) transform we have

$$\mathrm{E}[\log(Y_i)] = \beta_0 + \sum_{j=1}^{p} \beta_j x_{1ij} \tag{5.18}$$

$$\mathrm{V}[\log(Y_i)] = \exp\left(\gamma_0 + \sum_{j=1}^{q} \gamma_j x_{2ij}\right). \tag{5.19}$$

Thus a unit change in the jth independent variable in $\boldsymbol{x}_1$ gives a β_j change in the expected value of log(Y).

6. CONCLUSIONS

This monograph has barely begun to uncover the inferential and modeling potential given by an ML framework. The principle of maximum likelihood and the ML modeling framework discussed here provide us with the opportunity to build new and important bridges between social research and social theory. To make the most of this potential, however, we must have knowledge of the behavior and applicability of PDFs and PFs, along with the ability to construct models that correspond to that suggested by social theory. With a modeling approach based on the principle of maximum likelihood, we are able to specify link functions from the simplest linear model to much more complex nonlinear models.

Because of length considerations, important models that may be considered special cases of this framework (e.g., endogenous switching regression models and joint PDF/PF models) have not been discussed, nor have ML models for latent variables, or those for missing data. Unfortunately, a monograph of this size is not capable of giving adequate treatment to all the possibilities afforded us by an ML framework. It is my hope that future monographs in the QASS series will continue where this one has concluded.

APPENDIX: GAUSS CODE FOR SOME OF THE MODELS IN THE MONOGRAPH

The code given in this appendix includes three procedures for each ML model that may be used with the maximum likelihood procedures in Gauss. The first gives the code to calculate start values, the second is a procedure to calculate the log-likelihood for the model, and the third is a procedure to calculate the entropy-based dispersion measure. These three procedures can be interfaced with the Gauss maximum likelihood procedure. The appropriate interface protocol is discussed in the Gauss manual on ML procedures (Aptech Systems, 1992) and is not repeated here.

The Normal PDF Model

Procedure to Calculate Start Values

```
/* This procedure calculates start values for the
   Normal PDF Model. All variables should be
   globally declared before this procedure is
   called. All data is assumed to fit in memory,
```

```
   otherwise the procedure will have to be modified.
   There are no variables sent directly to the
   procedure; however, the following need to be
   assigned prior to calling this procedure.

   y  == column vector of observations for the
         endogenous random variable (the dependent
         variable)

   x1 == a matrix of fixed factors (independent
         variables) for the mu link function where
         rows are the cases and columns are the
         variables with the first column always
         being a column of ones

   x2 == a matrix of fixed factors (independent
         variables) for the sigma-squared link
         function where rows are the cases and
         columns are the variables with the first
         column always being a column of ones

   The procedure returns a column vector of start
   values in svs with as many rows as there are
   columns in x1 plus x2.

*/
proc strts;
         /*  initialize matrices */
         ij=cols(x1);
         xx = zeros(ij,ij);
         xy = zeros(ij,1);
         ybar = 0;
         yy = 0;
         obs = 0;
         bols = zeros(ij,1);

         /*  obtain sums of squares */
             obs = rows(y);
             xx = moment(x1,1);
             xy = (x1'y);
             yy = moment(y,1);

         /*  obtain OLS solution */
         bols = solpd(xy,xx);
         sigsqo = (yy-(xy'bols))./obs;
```

```
        clear xx,xy,yy;

        /*  concatenate start values in svs
        svs=bols|ln(sigsqo);
        if cols(x2) .> 1;
            svs=bols|ln(sigsqo)|zeros(cols(x2)-1,1);
        endif;

  retp( svs );
endp;
```

Procedure to Calculate the Log-likelihood

```
/* This procedure calculates the log-likelihood for
   the Normal PDF Model.

   Inputs:   b == column vector of parameters
             x == data matrix (number of cases by y~x1~x2)
                  (see start values for definition of y,
                   x1 and x2)

   Globals:  cx1 == number of columns in x1 (see start
                    values)

   Output:   lnl == column vector for the value of the
                    log-likelihood
*/
proc loglik(b,x);

        y = x[.,1];
        x1 = x[.,2:cx1+1];
        x2 = x[.,cx1+2:cols(x)];

        /* Link Functions */
        mu = x1*b[1:cols(x1),1];
        sigsq = exp(x2*b[1+cols(x1):rows(b),1]);

        /* Log-Likelihood */
        lnl = -0.5.*(ln(2.*pi.*sigsq)+(((y-mu).^2)
                                            ./sigsq));

        retp( lnl );

endp;
```

Procedure to Calculate Entropy-Based Measures

```
/* This proc calculates the entropy-based measures
   for the Normal Model. It expects that y, x1, and
   x2 are all defined as in the start values
   procedure and that the b contains the column
   vector of FINAL parameter estimates, the
   solution. This proc should only be called after a
   solution to the model is found. All data are
   expected to fit in memory, otherwise
   modifications will be needed.

             sst == total entropy
             sse == error or conditional entropy
             ssm == entropy accounted for by the model
             rent== entropy-based measure of association

*/
proc entropy;

        ybar=meanc(y);
        yvar=(moment(y,1)-((ybar.^2)./obs))./obs;
        p0 = (1./sqrt(2.*pi.*yvar)).*exp(-0.5.*(((y
                                      -ybar).^2)./yvar));
        sst = -sumc(ln(p0));

        mu = x1*b[1:cols(x1),1];
        sigsq = exp(x2*b[1+cols(x1):rows(b),1]);
        phat = (1./sqrt(2.*pi.*sigsq)).*exp(-0.5.*(((y
                                       -mu).^2)./sigsq));

        ssm=sumc(ln(phat./p0));
        sse=-sumc(ln(phat));
        rent=ssm./sst;

endp;
```

The Gamma PDF Model

Procedure to Calculate Start Values

```
/* This procedure calculates start values for the
   Gamma PDF Model. All variables should be globally
```

```
    declared before this procedure is called. All
    data is assumed to fit in memory, otherwise the
    procedure will have to be modified. There are no
    variables sent directly to the procedure;
    however, the following need to be assigned prior
    to calling this procedure.

    y == column vector of observations for the
          endogenous random variable (the dependent
          variable)

    x1 == a matrix of fixed factors (independent
          variables) for the mu link function where
          rows are the cases and columns are the
          variables with the first column always
          being a column of ones

    x2 == a matrix of fixed factors (independent
          variables) for the nu link function where
          rows are the cases and columns are the
          variables with the first column always
          being a column of ones

    The procedure returns a column vector of start
    values in svs with as many rows as there are
    columns in x1 plus x2.
*/
proc strts;

        /*  initialize matrices */
        ij=cols(x1);
        xx = zeros(ij,ij);
        xy = zeros(ij,1);
        yy = 0;
        obs = 0;
        bols = zeros(ij,1);

        /*  obtain sums of squares using ln(y) */
        obs = rows(y);
        xx = moment(x1,1);
        xy = x1'ln(y);
        yy = ln(y)'ln(y);
```

```
        /*  obtain OLS solution on ln(y) */
        bols = solpd(xy,xx);
        mu = exp(x1*bols);
        sigsq=sigsq+(((y-mu)./mu)'((y-mu)./mu));
        nuc = obs./sigsq;

        /*  concatenate start values */
        svs=bols|ln(nuc);
        if cols(x2) .> 1;
            svs=bols|ln(nuc)|zeros(cols(x2)-1,1);
        endif;

  retp( svs );
endp;
```

Procedure to Calculate the Log-Likelihood

```
/* This procedure calculates the log-likelihood for
   the Gamma PDF Model.

   Inputs:    b == column vector of parameters
              x == data matrix (number of cases by y~x1~x2)
                  (see start values for definition of y,
                   x1 and x2)

   Globals:   cx1 == number of columns in x1 (see start
                     values)

   Output:    lnl == column vector for the value of the
                     log-likelihood
*/
proc loglik(b,x);

        y = x[.,1];
        x1 = x[.,2:cx1+1];
        x2 = x[.,cx1+2:cols(x)];

        /* Link Functions */
        mu = exp(x1*b[1:cols(x1),1]);
        nu = exp(x2*b[1+cols(x1):rows(b),1]);

        /* Log-Likelihood */
        lnl = (-ln(gamma(nu))) + (nu.*ln(nu))
              - (nu.*ln(mu)) + ((nu-1).*ln(y))
```

```
            - ((nu./mu).*y);

        retp( lnl );

endp;
```

Procedure to Calculate Entropy-Based Measures

```
/* This proc calculates the entropy-based measures
   for the Gamma Model. It expects that y, x1, and
   x2 are all defined as in the start values
   procedure and that the b contains the column
   vector of FINAL parameter estimates, the
   solution. This proc should only be called after a
   solution to the model is found. All data are
   expected to fit in memory, otherwise
   modifications will be needed.
            sst == total entropy
            sse == error or conditional entropy
            ssm == entropy accounted for by the model
            rent== entropy-based measure of association
*/
proc entropy;

        obs=rows(y);
        yy0 = y'y;
        ybar=meanc(y);
        nu0 = obs./((yy0./(ybar.^2))-(2.*obs)
                                        +(obs.^2));
        lp0 = (-ln(gamma(nu0)))+(nu0.*ln(nu0))
              -(nu0.*ln(ybar))+((nu0-1).*ln(y))
              -((nu0./ybar).*y);
        sst = -sumc(lp0);

        mu = exp(x1*b[1:cols(x1),1]);
        nu = exp(x2*b[1+cols(x1):rows(b),1]);
        lphat = (-ln(gamma(nu)))+(nu.*ln(nu))
                -(nu.*ln(mu))+((nu-1).*ln(y))
                -((nu./mu).*y);

        ssm=sumc(lphat-lp0);
        sse=-sumc(lphat);
        rent=ssm./sst;

endp;
```

The Multinomial PF Model

Procedure to Calculate Start Values

```
/* This procedure calculates start values for the
   Multinomial PF Model. All variables should be
   globally declared before this procedure is
   called. All data is assumed to fit in memory,
   otherwise the procedure will have to be modified.
   There are no variables sent directly to the
   procedure; however, the following need to be
   assigned prior to calling this procedure.

   yvec == column vector of observations for the
         endogenous random variable (the dependent
         variable) containing an integer
         representing the category in which each
         observation may be found

   x  == a matrix of fixed factors (independent
         variables) for the J-1 p link functions
         where rows are the cases and columns are
         the variables with the first column always
         being a column of ones

   The procedure returns a column vector of start
   values in svs with rows equal to cols(x)*(J-1).
*/
proc strts;
        /*  obtain start values from OLS estimators
            with marginal log-odds ratio on last
            category as dependent variables */

        kh=cols(x);
        h=maxc(y)-1;
        y= yvec .== (seqa(1,1,h)');
        xx=moment(x,1);
        xy=x'y;
        pmarg=sumc(y);
        obs=rows(y);
        pmarg=pmarg./obs;
        pmargl=1-sumc(pmarg);
        dv=ln(pmarg/pmargl);
        vc=(eye(h)-pmarg).*pmarg';
        invvc=invpd(vc);
```

```
        dl=pmarg-vc*dv;
        invm=invpd(xx);
        bmls=invm*xy;
        vv=zeros(kh,h);
        vv[1,.]=ones(1,h).*(dl');
        bm=((bmls-vv)*invvc);
        svs=vec(bm);
        retp(svs);
endp;
```

Procedure to Calculate the Log-Likelihood

```
/* This procedure calculates the log-likelihood for
   the Multinomial Model.

   Inputs:   b == column vector of parameters
             yx == data matrix (number of cases by yvec~x)
                  (see start values for definition of
                   yvec and x)

   Globals:  h == number of categories in yvec minus 1

   Output:   lnl == column vector for the value of the
                    log-likelihood
*/
proc loglik(b,yx);

        y= yx[.,1] .== (seqa(1,1,h)');
        x = yx[.,2:cols(yx)];
        kh=cols(x);

        /* Link Functions */
        bm=reshape(b,h,kh)';
        p = exp(x*bm);
        p = p./(1+sumc(p'));

        /* Log-Likelihood */
        lnl=sumc(sumc((ln(p~(1-sumc(p')))).*(y~(1
                                              -sumc(y')))')');

        retp( lnl );
endp;
```

Procedure to Calculate Entropy-Based Measures

```
/* This proc calculates the entropy-based measures
   for the Multinomial Model. It expects that yvec,
   x, pmarg, kh, and h are all defined as in proc
   strts and that the b contains the column vector
   of FINAL parameter estimates, the solution. This
   proc should only be called after a solution to
   the model is found. All data are expected to fit
   in memory, otherwise modifications will be needed.
              sst == total entropy
              sse == error or conditional entropy
              ssm == entropy accounted for by the model
              rent== entropy-based measure of association
*/
proc entropy;

         /* calculate the total entropy */
         sst = obs.*(sumc((-1).*pmarg.*ln(pmarg))-
                    ((1-sumc(pmarg)).*ln(1-sumc(pmarg))));

         /* calculate the conditional (error) entropy */
         x = yx[.,2:cols(yx)];
         bm=reshape(b,h,kh)';
         p = exp(x*bm);
         p = p./(1+sumc(p'));
         clear ssei;
         ssei = (-1.0).*(1-sumc(p')).*ln((1-sumc(p')));
         jj=1;
         do until jj > h;
             sseei = sseei + ((-1.0).*p[.,jj].*
                                            ln(p[.,jj])) ;
             jj=jj+1;
         endo;
         sse = sumc(sseei);
         ssm = sst-sse;
         rent = ssm./sst;

endp;
```

The Bivariate Normal PDF Model

Procedure to Calculate Start Values

```
/* This procedure calculates start values for the
   Bivariate Normal PDF Model. All variables should
   be globally declared before this procedure is
   called. All data is assumed to fit in memory,
   otherwise the procedure will have to be modified.
   There are no variables sent directly to the
   procedure; however, the following need to be
   assigned prior to calling this procedure.

   y1 == column vector of observations for the first
         endogenous random variable (dependent
         variable)

   y2 == column vector of observations for the
         second endogenous random variable
         (dependent variable)

   x1 == a matrix of fixed factors (independent
         variables) for the mu1 link function where
         rows are the cases and columns are the
         variables with the first column always
         being a column of ones

   x2 == a matrix of fixed factors (independent
         variables) for the mu2 link function where
         rows are the cases and columns are the
         variables with the first column always
         being a column of ones

   x3 == a matrix of fixed factors (independent
         variables) for the sigma-squared-1 link
         function where rows are the cases and
         columns are the variables with the first
         column always being a column of ones

   x4 == a matrix of fixed factors (independent
         variables) for the sigma-squared-2 link
         function where rows are the cases and
         columns are the variables with the first
         column always being a column of ones
```

```
   x5 == a matrix of fixed factors (independent
         variables) for the rho link function where
         rows are the cases and columns are the
         variables with the first column always
         being a column of ones

   The procedure returns a column vector of start
   values in svs with as many rows as there are
   columns in x1+x2+x3+x4+x5.
*/
proc strts;
        /* initialize matrices */
        ij1=cols(x1);ij2=cols(x2);
        xx1 = zeros(ij1,ij1);xy1 = zeros(ij1,1);
        xx2 = zeros(ij2,ij2);xy2 = zeros(ij2,1);
        cor0=0;corr=0;
        y1bar = 0;y2bar = 0;
        y1var = 0;y2var = 0;
        y1y2 = 0;
        yy1 = 0;yy2 = 0;
        obs = 0;
        bols1 = zeros(ij1,1);bols2 = zeros(ij2,1);

        /* obtain the sums of squares */
        obs = rows(y1);
        xx1 = moment(x1,1);
        xx2 = moment(x2,1);
        xy1 = x1'y1;
        xy2 = x2'y2;
        y1y2 = y1'y2;
        yy1 = moment(y1,1);
        yy2 = moment(y2,1);
        y1bar=meanc(y1);
        y2bar=meanc(y2);

        /* obtain the OLS estimates */
        bols1 = solpd(xy1,xx1);
        bols2 = solpd(xy2,xx2);
        sigsq1 = (yy1-(xy1'bols1))./obs;
        sigsq2 = (yy2-(xy2'bols2))./obs;
        mu1 = x1*bols1;
        mu2 = x2*bols2;
        corr= (y1-mu1)'(y2-mu2);
```

```
        corr=(corr./obs)./sqrt(sigsq1.*sigsq2);

        /*  concatenate start values */
        svs=bols1|bols2|ln(sigsq1);
        if cols(x3) .> 1;
             svs=svs|zeros(cols(x3)-1,1);
        endif;
        svs=svs|ln(sigsq2);
        if cols(x4) .> 1;
             svs=svs|zeros(cols(x4)-1,1);
        endif;
        if corparm .< 1;
             svs=svs|ln((1+corr)./(1-corr));
             if cols(x5) .> 1;
                svs=svs|zeros(cols(x5)-1,1);
             endif;
        endif;

  retp( svs );
endp;
```

Procedure to Calculate the Log-Likelihood

```
/* This procedure calculates the log-likelihood for
   the Bivariate Normal Model.

   Inputs:    b == column vector of parameters
              x == data matrix (number of cases by
                                 y1~y2~x1~x2~x3~x4~x5)
                   (see start values for definition of
                    y1, y2, x1, x2, x3, x4, and x5)

   Globals:   k1 == number of columns in x1 (see start
                    values)
              k2 == number of columns in x2 (see start
                    values)
              k3 == number of columns in x3 (see start
                    values)
              k4 == number of columns in x4 (see start
                    values)
              k5 == number of columns in x5 (see start
                    values)

   Output:    lnl == column vector for the value of the
                     log-likelihood
```

```
*/
proc loglik(b,x);
        y1=x[.,1];y2=x[.,2];x=x[.,3:cols(x)];
        x1=x[.,1:k1];x=x[.,k1+1,cols(x)];
        x2=x[.,1:k2];x=x[.,k2+1,cols(x)];
        x3=x[.,1:k3];x=x[.,k3+1,cols(x)];
        x4=x[.,1:k4];
        x5=x[.,k4+1,cols(x)];

        k1=cols(x1);k2=k1+cols(x2);k3=k2+cols(x3);
        k4=k3+cols(x4);k5=k4+cols(x5);
        mu1 = x1*b[1:k1,1];
        mu2 = x2*b[k1+1:k2,1];
        sigsq1=exp(x3*b[k2+1:k3,1]);
        sigsq2=exp(x4*b[k3+1:k4,1]);
        corr= (exp(x5*b[k4+1:k5,1])-1)./
                            (exp(x5*b[k4+1:k5,1])+1);

        lnl = -ln(2.*pi.*sqrt(sigsq1.*sigsq2.*(1
              -corr.^2))) + ((-1./(2.*(1-corr.^2))).*
              ((((y1-mu1).^2)./sigsq1) - (2.*corr.*
              ((y1-mu1)./sqrt(sigsq1)).*((y2-mu2)./
              sqrt(sigsq2))) + (((y2-mu2).^2)./
              sigsq2) ));

        retp( lnl );

endp;
```

Procedure to Calculate Entropy-Based Measures

```
/* This proc calculates the entropy-based measures
   for the Gamma Model. It expects that y1, y2, and
   x1-x5 are all defined as in the proc strts and
   that the b contains the column vector of FINAL
   parameter estimates, the solution. This proc
   should only be called after a solution to the
   model is found. All data are expected to fit in
   memory, otherwise modifications will be needed.
             sst == total entropy
             sse == error or conditional entropy
             ssm == entropy accounted for by the model
             rent== entropy-based measure of association
*/
proc entropy;
```

```
        y1y2 = y1'y2;
        yy1 = moment(y1,1);
        yy2 = moment(y2,1);
        y1bar=sumc(y1);
        y2bar=sumc(y2);
        obs=rows(y1);
        cor0 = (y1y2 - ((y1bar.*y2bar)./obs))./
               sqrt( (yy1-((y1bar.^2)./obs)).*(yy2-
               ((y2bar.^2)./obs)) );
        y1var=(yy1-((y1bar.^2)./obs))./obs;
        y2var=(yy2-((y2bar.^2)./obs))./obs;
        y1bar=y1bar./obs;
        y2bar=y2bar./obs;

        p0 = (1./(2.*pi.*sqrt(y1var.*y2var.*(1-
             cor0.^2)))).*exp((-1./(2.*(1-
             cor0.^2))).*((((y1-y1bar).^2)./y1var) -
             (2.*cor0.*((y1-y1bar)./sqrt(y1var)).*
             ((y2-y2bar)./sqrt(y2var))) +
             (((y2-y2bar).^2)./y2var)));

        sst = -sumc(ln(p0));

        k1=cols(x1);k2=k1+cols(x2);k3=k2+cols(x3);
        k4=k3+cols(x4);k5=k4+cols(x5);
        mu1 = x1*b[1:k1,1];
        mu2 = x2*b[k1+1:k2,1];
        sigsq1=exp(x3*b[k2+1:k3,1]);
        sigsq2=exp(x4*b[k3+1:k4,1]);

        corr= (exp(x5*b[k4+1:k5,1])-1)./(exp(x5*b[k4
              +1:k5,1])+1);

        phat= (1./(2.*pi.*sqrt(sigsq1.*sigsq2.*(1-
              corr.^2)))).*exp((-1./(2.*(1-
              corr.^2))).*((((y1-mu1).^2)./sigsq1) -
              (2.*corr.*((y1-mu1)./sqrt(sigsq1)).*
              ((y2-mu2)./sqrt(sigsq2))) +
              (((y2-mu2).^2)./sigsq2)));

        ssm=sumc(ln(phat./p0));
        sse=-sume(ln(phat));
        rent=ssm./sst;

endp;
```

NOTES

1. Fisher referred to this function as the "probability of the sample" for fixed $\boldsymbol{\theta}$. See Stuart and Ord (1991, vol. 2) for details.

2. It is usually not specified how large a sample size is "large enough." For models with few parameters to estimate (i.e., 1 to about 5), a sample size of more than 60 is usually large enough. This issue is better cast in terms of degrees of freedom, because how large is "large enough" depends on the number of estimable parameters in the model and the probability of committing a Type I error, usually denoted as the α level. Thus, at $\alpha = 0.05$ for a two-tailed testing situation, degrees of freedom of at least 60 for well-behaved models is usually good enough. Why? At 60 degrees of freedom and $\alpha = 0.05$ (two-tailed), Student's t distribution and the standard unit normal give values of 2.00 and 1.96, respectively. For those who wish to be more conservative, degrees of freedom of at least 120 give an even better approximation, with values of 1.98 and 1.96, respectively.

3. These results assume that the number of estimated parameters either remain constant as N tends toward infinity, or, if the number of parameters also increases with N, that N tends toward infinity at a sufficiently faster rate than do the number of estimated parameters, so that the ratio of N to the number of parameters also tends toward infinity with N.

4. This is not the same, however, as choosing that hypothesis with the highest probability of occurrence. See Stuart and Ord (1991, vol. 1) for details and discussion.

5. A note of caution is appropriate at this point. When conducting hypothesis tests such as those described here, it is a violation of the testing structure to use data first to ascertain possible restrictions on the parameter space and then to use those same data to test those restrictions. One cannot do this and retain the distributions expected under the null hypothesis for the test. The logic of the test procedure breaks down, the distribution of the test statistic under the null hypothesis is affected, the Type I error rate becomes inflated, and the test in general becomes invalid. It should be noted further that these cautions apply to all hypothesis-testing situations, not just those described by the procedure above. In general, it is inappropriate to test the fit, accuracy, or behavior of parameters in structural models when knowledge of the existence of those parameters in the model is obtained from exploration of the patterns in the data themselves. In a strict sense, the hypothesis tests should be derived from information that is independent of the data to be used for the test. See Hurvich and Tsai (1990) for details.

6. However, the work of Clogg, Petkova, and Shihadeh (1992) appears promising with respect to developing such a test statistic in this context.

REFERENCES

AGRESTI, A. (1990) Categorical Data Analysis. New York: John Wiley.

ALBA, R. D. (1988) "Interpreting the parameters of log-linear models," in J. S. Long (ed.) Common Problems/Proper Solutions: Avoiding Error in Quantitative Research. Newbury Park, CA: Sage.

AMEMIYA, T. (1985) Advanced Econometrics. Cambridge, MA: Harvard University Press.

Aptech Systems (1992) The Gauss System Version 3.0. Kent, WA: Author.

BERNDT, E., HALL, B., HALL, R., and HAUSMAN, J. (1974) "Estimation and inference in nonlinear structural models." Annals of Economic and Social Measurement 3: 653-665.

BISHOP, Y. M. M., FIENBERG, S. E., and HOLLAND, P. W. (1975) Discrete Multivariate Analysis: Theory and Practice. Cambridge: MIT Press.

Center for Human Resource Research, Ohio State University (1988) National Longitudinal Surveys of Labor Market Experience. Columbus: Author.

CLOGG, C. C., PETKOVA, E., and SHIHADEH, E. S. (1992) "Statistical methods for analyzing collapsibility in regression models." Journal of Educational Statistics 17: 51-74.

CLOGG, C. C., and SHOCKEY, J. W. (1988) "Multivariate analysis of discrete data," in J. R. Nesselroade and R. B. Cattell (eds.) Handbook of Multivariate Experimental Psychology. New York: Plenum.

COLEMAN, J. S. (1990) Foundations of Social Theory. Cambridge, MA: Belknap.

CRAMER, J. S. (1986) Econometric Applications of Maximum Likelihood Methods. Cambridge: Cambridge University Press.

DENNIS, J. E., Jr., and SCHNABEL, R. B. (1983) Numerical Methods for Unconstrained Optimization and Nonlinear Equations. Englewood Cliffs, NJ: Prentice-Hall.

FIENBERG, S. E. (1977) The Analysis of Cross-Classified Categorical Data. Cambridge: MIT Press.

FISHER, R. A. (1950) Contributions to Mathematical Statistics. New York: Wiley.

GOLDTHORPE, J. H. (1987) Social Mobility and Class Structure in Modern Britain. Oxford: Clarendon.

GOODMAN, L. A. (1978) Analyzing Qualitative/Categorical Data. New York: University Press of America.

GREENE, W. H. (1993) Econometric Analysis (2nd ed.). New York: Macmillan.

HABERMAN, S. J. (1978a) Analysis of Qualitative Data, Vol. 1: Introductory Topics. New York: Academic Press.

HABERMAN, S. J. (1978b) Analysis of Qualitative Data, Vol. 2: New Developments. New York: Academic Press.

HABERMAN, S. J. (1982) "Analysis of dispersion of multinomial responses." Journal of the American Statistical Association 77: 568-580.

HURVICH, C. M., and TSAI, C. (1990) "The impact of model selection on inference in linear regression." American Statistician 44: 214-217.

JASSO, G. (1990) "Methods for the theoretical and empirical analysis of comparison processes." Sociological Methodology 20: 369-420.

KING, G. (1989) Unifying Political Methodology. Cambridge: Cambridge University Press.

LONG, J. S. (1984) "Estimable functions in log-linear models." Sociological Methods & Research 12: 399-432.

LONG, J. S. (1987) "A graphical method for the interpretation of multinomial logit analysis." Sociological Methods & Research 15:420-446.

LUENBERGER, D. G. (1984) Linear and Nonlinear Programming. Reading, MA: Addison-Wesley.

MADDALA, G. S. (1983) Limited-Dependent and Qualitative Variables in Econometrics. Cambridge: Cambridge University Press.

McCULLAGH, P., and NELDER, J. A. (1989) Generalized Linear Models (2nd ed.). London: Chapman & Hall.

NETER, J., WASSERMAN, W., and KUTNER, M. H. (1985) Applied Linear Regression Models (2nd ed.). Homewood, IL: Irwin.

ROEMER, J. (1986) Analytical Marxism. Cambridge: Cambridge University Press.

SCHNEIDER, H. (1986) Truncated and Censored Samples From Normal Populations. New York: Marcel Dekker.

SHANNON, C. E. (1948) "A mathematical theory of communication." Bell System Technical Journal 27: 379-423, 623-656.

SOBEL, M. E. (1993a) "Causal inference in the social and behavioral sciences," in G. Arminger, C. C. Clogg, and M. E. Sobel (eds.) A Handbook for Statistical Modeling in the Social and Behavioral Sciences. New York: Plenum.

SOBEL, M. E. (1993b) "Log-linear models," in G. Arminger, C. C. Clogg, and M. E. Sobel (eds.) A Handbook for Statistical Modeling in the Social and Behavioral Sciences. New York: Plenum.

STRYKER, R. (1992) "What's an administrator of law to do? Law, science, and the legitimacy of the welfare state." Unpublished manuscript.

STUART, A., and ORD, J. K. (1991) Kendall's advanced theory of statistics (Vols. 1-2, 5th ed.). New York: Oxford University Press.

THISTED, R. A. (1988) Elements of Statistical Computing: Numerical Computation. New York: Chapman & Hall.

WRIGHT, E. O. (1985) Classes. London: Verso.

ABOUT THE AUTHOR

SCOTT R. ELIASON is Assistant Professor of Sociology at the University of Iowa, where he teaches courses in quantitative methods and social stratification. He is currently Director of the university's Modular Topics in Methods and Statistics. He holds a Ph.D. from the Pennsylvania State University. His primary substantive work is in the areas of the sociology of occupations, labor markets, social status, and social class. He is also active in the area of advanced statistics in the social sciences, with emphasis on the analysis of categorical data and the relationship between theory construction and statistical analysis.